HOPE

DR. DAVID JEREMIAH

HOPE

LIVING FEARLESSLY
in a SCARY WORLD

TYNDALE
MOMENTUM®

The Tyndale nonfiction imprint

Visit Tyndale online at tyndale.com.

Visit Tyndale Momentum online at tyndalemomentum.com.

TYNDALE, Tyndale's quill logo, *Tyndale Momentum*, and the Tyndale Momentum logo are registered trademarks of Tyndale House Ministries. Tyndale Momentum is the nonfiction imprint of Tyndale House Publishers, Carol Stream, Illinois.

Hope: Living Fearlessly in a Scary World

Copyright © 2021 by David Jeremiah. All rights reserved.

Adapted from *What Are You Afraid Of?*, published in 2013 by Tyndale House Publishers under ISBN 978-1-4143-8046-9.

Cover photograph of pathway copyright © asefyan/iStockphoto. All rights reserved.

Cover photograph of flowerbeds copyright © Julia Kuleshova/Shutterstock. All rights reserved.

Cover photograph of sunlight copyright © givaga/Shutterstock. All rights reserved.

Author photograph taken by Alan Weissman, copyright © 2013. All rights reserved.

Designed by Chris Gilbert at Gearbox Studios

Edited by Stephanie Rische

Published in association with Yates & Yates (www.yates2.com).

All Scripture quotations, unless otherwise indicated, are taken from the New King James Version.® Copyright © 1982 by Thomas Nelson, Inc. Used by permission. All rights reserved.

Scripture quotations marked KJV are taken from the *Holy Bible*, King James Version.

Scripture quotations marked *The Message* are taken from *The Message* by Eugene H. Peterson, copyright © 1993, 1994, 1995, 1996, 2000, 2001, 2002. Used by permission of NavPress Publishing Group. All rights reserved.

Scripture quotations marked NIV are taken from the Holy Bible, *New International Version*,® *NIV*.® Copyright © 1973, 1978, 1984, 2011 by Biblica, Inc.® Used by permission. All rights reserved worldwide.

For information about special discounts for bulk purchases, please contact Tyndale House Publishers at csresponse@tyndale.com, or call 1-800-323-9400.

ISBN 978-1-4143-8047-6

Printed in the United States of America

27	26	25	24	23	22	21
7	6	5	4	3	2	1

Dr. Ken Nichols is a biblical counselor and communicator whose friendship and partnership in ministry reach back more than thirty-five years. Wherever he has been, you will find people whose lives have been healed because of his ministry. Over the last several years, we have talked often about the subject of fear, and he was the first to suggest that I write a book on the topic.

Here it is, Ken. It is dedicated to you.

Thank you for your encouragement!

Contents

Introduction

You are asleep in your bed when your alarm shocks you awake. You pick up your phone and see the headlines filled with news of approaching thunderstorms, overnight killings, fires, stock-market plunges, government scandals, and car wrecks. Instead of jumping out of bed, you pull the covers up over your head. You know what a fearful world we live in, and you dread facing all the challenges of the day.

But maybe your morning fears are not in the news; they're about your job. You live in constant fear of getting caught in the downsizing trend. Or you're apprehensive about a business deal that has your career on the line.

Maybe your deepest fears lie at home. Can you meet this month's mortgage payment? Does your marriage seem shaky? Are your kids worrying you? After a recent service at the church I pastor in Southern California, a young soldier who had just returned from Afghanistan wept as he asked me to pray for him. He feared that he might be losing his family.

Might. That's the word that's haunting him. Our greatest

fear is the conditional might—the threat of what *might* happen. Fear trades in the market of possibility. Or even impossibility—for fear is the tyrant of the imagination. It imposes itself upon us from the shadows, from its hazy mirror of maybe.

There's no question about it: we live in a world that is often a scary place to be. When we face these fears that prompt us to pull the covers over our heads and retreat from the world, what will we put our hope in? Will we exert our energy in wishful thinking, crossing our fingers that our circumstances will change? Will we hold our breath in the hope that luck will go our way this time?

Biblical hope is not wishful thinking. It's not a lucky chance. It's not ungrounded optimism. No, it's a rock-solid belief in the character of God. That's not to say we are guaranteed rosebushes without thorns or a life free from tragedy or disaster. But because we know that God is all-knowing and all-powerful and for us, we can face down our fears and trust the outcome of our circumstances to Him.

Hebrews 11:1 says, "Now faith is the substance of things hoped for, the evidence of things not seen." The antidote to fear is faith. And faith gives us hope in the midst of whatever scary thing we face. When the apostle Paul was giving counsel to Timothy, his young protégé, he knew Timothy was afraid of something—probably of his assignment to lead the large church in Ephesus. Timothy was raised in a small town in Asia Minor, and Ephesus was the big city. Paul himself had spent three years in Ephesus, building up the church there.

It was led by a strong group of elders, yet false teachers were causing trouble. And Timothy was supposed to go in and be the leader of the whole thing. What young pastor wouldn't have felt fear at the prospect?

So what did Paul tell Timothy? "Your fear is not from God. What do come from God are power, love, and a stable mental attitude" (2 Timothy 1:7, my paraphrase).

Paul knew that when we get God's perspective on the source of our fear, we can set aside what is not from Him and embrace what is. In all my years of following Christ, studying the Bible, and pastoring well-intentioned Christians, I have yet to find a fear for which God does not have an answer. And the reason is simple: God Himself is the answer to all our fears.

Think about it—fear is almost always based on the future. Sometimes we're afraid because we know what's coming in the future. But more commonly, we're afraid of what we don't know about the future. We're afraid of what might happen. For instance, the Gallup organization asked thirteen- to seventeen-year-olds what they were most afraid of. In descending order, the top ten fears of these teens were terrorist attacks, spiders, death/being killed, not succeeding in life/being a failure, war, heights, crime/violence, being alone, the future, and nuclear war.[1]

Notice that all these fears are future focused, and all are merely "maybes." These teens may encounter none of them. Whether the future is just a minute from now (you're waiting on a doctor's diagnosis) or five years from now (you worry about having enough money for retirement), fear's home office is the future.

But what is the future to God? To Him the future is now! We live inside time while God, who made it, lives outside it. We know relatively little about the future, while God knows everything about it. All the events in our lives occur in two time frames: past and future. (The present is a continuously fleeing, infinitesimal moment that becomes past even before we can define it.) God, on the other hand, has only one frame of reference: the eternal now, in which He sees and knows everything, including the future.

That's why God is the answer to all our fears. If God is good and loving (and He is), and if God is all-powerful (and He is), and if God has a purpose and a plan that include His children (and He does), and if we are His children (as I hope you are), then there is no reason to fear and every reason to hope, for God is in control of everything.

I know—that's good theology, and you probably believe it. But you still have fears and apprehensions and a hollow place in the pit of your stomach, either sometimes or all the time. The great author Edith Wharton once said that she didn't believe in ghosts, but she was afraid of them. It's one thing to know something with the mind, and another to believe it with the heart.

How do you help a little child face her fear of the darkness? First you appeal to the mind. You turn on the light and show her there's nothing scary in the room. Then you help her attune her heart to what her mind has accepted. This is the process of faith, for all of us. We accept that God is in control, and on that basis, we shift our burdens to His perfect shoulders.

But what about our shaky future? Pessimism doesn't work, because it's another form of mental enslavement. Optimism may have no basis in reality. The one way to walk with hope and confidence into an unknown future is to stake everything on the power and goodness and faithfulness of God.

To understand why God is the answer to all our fears, we must understand what the Bible says about fear. And it says a lot. It tells us more than three hundred times not to fear. "Fear not" is its most frequently repeated command. The word *afraid* occurs more than two hundred times, and *fear* more than four hundred. And lest you think our Bible heroes were fearless, more than two hundred individuals in Scripture are said to have been afraid. And not all these were the "bad guys"; many were the main characters—David, Paul, Timothy, and others.

Biblical heroes were regular people who had to learn the same things you and I have to learn—to drive out fear by increasing their knowledge of God, to shift their focus from their present fear to their eternal hope, to replace what they didn't know about the future with what they did know about Him. They had to put away childish things (being afraid of everything) and grow up in their faith and understanding.

I wrote this book because I see fear as a real and present danger in the body of Christ. Many Christians are not living lives free of fear, and there can be serious consequences when hope is absent.

Jesus came to "proclaim liberty to the captives," and I believe that includes those held captive by fear (Luke 4:18). He also says that truth is the key to freedom (John 8:32). And here is the truth: God is good (Psalm 119:68), God is love (1 John 4:8, 16), and God has a future filled with hope for His children (Jeremiah 29:11; Romans 8:28-29). God is a refuge and a fortress, a shield and a defender for those who trust in Him (Psalm 91:2-4). For those reasons, and more . . .

> *You shall not be afraid of the terror by night,*
> *Nor of the arrow that flies by day,*
> *Nor of the pestilence that walks in darkness,*
> *Nor of the destruction that lays waste at noonday.*
> *A thousand may fall at your side,*
> *And ten thousand at your right hand;*
> *But it shall not come near you.*
>
> PSALM 91:5-7

As you read this book, my prayers are that you will grow in your conviction that God is the answer to all your fears, that as you look to the future you will see nothing except His power and love guarding your every step, and that you will find the truth that sets you free to live the hope-filled life God created you to enjoy.

CHAPTER 1

HOPE IN THE MIDST OF THE STORM

*Do not be afraid of sudden terror, nor of trouble
from the wicked when it comes.*

PROVERBS 3:25

When the *Andrea Gail* left Gloucester Harbor in Massachusetts on September 20, 1991, and headed into the North Atlantic, no one could have known that this fishing boat would never be seen again. Only a bit of debris ever turned up, and the six crew members vanished forever.

In his book *The Perfect Storm*, author Sebastian Junger immortalized the fate of the *Andrea Gail*. A film followed, featuring George Clooney and Mark Wahlberg. But these stars, big as they are, played only supporting roles. The real star was the storm itself—a terrifying, relentless oppressor born of fierce wind and mountainous waves.

It was meteorologists who named this cataclysmic tempest

"the perfect storm." I might not tend to use the word *perfect* to describe something so terrible, but once you understand the meteorologist's usage, "perfect storm" makes perfect sense. It is merely a vivid way of saying "worst-case scenario." In the case of the *Andrea Gail,* it was the simultaneous occurrence of the toughest weather conditions possible.

Three deadly elements came together in October of 1991: a front moving from Canada toward New England; a high pressure system building over Canada's east coast; and the dying remnants of Hurricane Grace, churning along the eastern seaboard of the United States. Strong weather was coming from three of the four points on the compass, all of it converging on the little *Andrea Gail.*

On their own, warm air, cold air, and moist air are hardly noticeable. But when wind patterns force them together, the result can be lethal. The last radio transmission of Billy Tyne, the captain of the fishing boat, came at 6:00 p.m. on October 28, 1991. He reported his coordinates to the captain of his sister ship, the *Hannah Boden,* saying, "She's comin' on, boys, and she's comin' on strong."[1]

The popular book and movie brought the term "perfect storm" into common usage, but the concept is as old as humanity. People have always had to deal with the convergence of multiple rough circumstances. So much can go wrong so quickly that we shake our heads and say, "When it rains, it pours."

We've all been there, haven't we? Your child gets sick, and your car breaks down on the way to the doctor. All the while it's pouring rain, and your spouse isn't answering the phone. One or two of these difficulties aren't so bad, but when they arrive together, they can form quite a storm.

As frustrating as such storms can be, much worse can happen. Today, in our faster, more crowded, and more complex world, a few little squalls can quickly become "the perfect storm." When multiple conditions converge and threaten critical areas of our lives, such as finances, relationships, jobs, and health, we question how much more we can endure. Somewhere there's a point at which we reach critical mass. Once there, we wonder whether we will stay afloat or go under like the *Andrea Gail*. Knowing that could happen strikes fear into us.

The fate of the *Andrea Gail* demonstrates two specific kinds of fear that we all experience. The first is that gut-level, adrenaline-drenched fear that the crew felt in the midst of the storm. They were afraid because their lives were on the line. This kind of fear is beneficial; it's a necessary instinct for survival. No doubt the fishermen of the North Atlantic feel a little surge of that fear every time they leave port. One poor decision in the face of threatening weather could mean death. But that doesn't stop these men and women. Reasonable fear is a healthy, normal part of the job description. If they couldn't handle it, they'd be in some other line of work.

But there's another kind of fear that can immobilize us completely: the fear of fear itself. Fear in the midst of the storm is instinctive and beneficial. Fear of a storm that *could* happen is not. It's an intrusive emotion that can lead us to a greatly diminished life. The imagined fear becomes so vivid that we no longer distinguish it from reality, and for some of us, that fear becomes so debilitating we can hardly get out of bed in the morning. Though the sky is clear, we're devastated by thoughts of rain. Inside a storm, at least we can look the beast in the eye. But with the fear of fear, the imagined monster is always just on the other side of the door, looming large, even though it doesn't exist.

Everyone must face fear, but for the believer, its fangs are drawn in because we are protected by an overarching umbrella of hope. Nonbelievers must contrive coping mechanisms, all of which are ineffective. Fatalism ("we're all doomed") doesn't work. Existentialism ("we're all clueless") leads nowhere. Optimism ("hey, it's all good") lets us down because it's a lie. It's *not* all good. There are things in life worth fearing.

We need a perspective on fear that takes into account the perfect storms of life but also reassures us that there's a safe harbor within reach. We can't put away all fear, but we need not live as its slaves.

That's where Jesus Christ comes in. As we put our hope in Him, this world and its emotions look different in the light of His goodness, power, and wisdom. Fear is simply a fact we must deal with in a fallen universe, but in the Bible we learn that fear can be managed. In God's Word there is a wealth of guidance on dealing with storms, perfect and imperfect.

The Probability of Storms in Our Lives

When evening had come, [Jesus] said to them, "Let us cross over to the other side." Now when they had left the multitude, they took Him along in the boat as He was. And other little boats were also with Him. And a great windstorm arose, and the waves beat into the boat, so that it was already filling.

MARK 4:35-37

Matthew, Mark, and Luke all relay the story of a perfect storm in the lives of Jesus' disciples. On that night a quiet boat ride turned into a terrifying brush with death. While Matthew (8:23-27) and Luke (8:22-25) cover the basic facts, Mark's version of the event is the most detailed (4:1, 35-41).

The Gospels record that Jesus was near exhaustion, and His twelve disciples were reeling from the rigorous training He'd been giving them. The crowds had been overwhelming. Sick people, craving His healing touch, had flocked to Jesus on every street. The disciples stood in awe of their Master's miracles and were astonished that He expected them to perform miracles too. Their lives were being turned inside out.

Now Jesus was speaking near the shore of the Sea of Galilee. The crowds began to press in so hard that He was almost shoved back into the water. He climbed into a boat, pushed out a few feet, sat down, and continued teaching (Mark 4:1). By the time He had finished, it was evening. Since Mark devotes almost thirty verses to the event, it must have been a significant teaching session, lasting several hours. Jesus must have been exhausted. The crowd, however, was not about to leave. Desperately needing rest, Jesus and the disciples simply remained in the boat and set sail for the eastern shore, where Jesus sought to minister next.

The elements of a perfect storm were gathering. First, Jesus was utterly exhausted (Mark 4:38). Second, the disciples, too, were tired and emotionally befuddled by their extraordinary experiences with Jesus. Third, it was already nighttime—late to be setting out to cross the sea. Fourth, a small flotilla of eager followers was trailing them, meaning that when they landed, rest would remain elusive.

Then there was the sea itself. The Sea of Galilee is like a bowl of water nestled nearly seven hundred feet below sea level. It is both fed and drained by the Jordan River, which enters at the northern end and exits from the southern end. Mountains flank nearly every side, forming valleys and gullies that set the stage for howling winds. When the cool air from the mountains swoops through the valleys and collides with the warm, moist air hovering over the sea, violent storms can erupt in a matter of minutes.

And that is just what happened. "A great windstorm arose, and the waves beat into the boat, so that it was already filling" (Mark 4:37). Mark uses a Greek word for *windstorm* that can be translated "furious squall" or "hurricane." Matthew describes the storm as a "great *seismos*," or earthquake—as if the sea were being shaken by the winds (Matthew 8:24).

Fatigue. Confusion. Darkness. Tempest. The perfect storm

had arrived. It was as if all their fears had combined and crystallized. As fishermen, they had a deep, fearful respect for the turbulent water. As men, they had a deep but relatively untested respect for Jesus. But now this Jesus—the One they had left everything to follow—had led them right into the storm. To make matters worse, He had dozed off, having no apparent concern for their safety or the disaster that now seemed inevitable. They must have wondered whether they had taken the right step in following Him. There was a lot they still didn't know about this man. Could He even deliver them from the disaster that now seemed inevitable?

Just as sudden storms are inevitable on the Sea of Galilee, sudden storms can descend upon our lives as well. When this happens, the disciples' predicament becomes ours: How is it possible to place your hope in a God who allows perfect storms to assail us?

The Paradox of Storms in Our Lives

The disciples were following Jesus wherever He went, assisting Him in all His ministries. They were listening to His Word and helping Him preach the Gospel, yet they found themselves being tossed up and down by a storm and in real danger of drowning. The disciples were learning a difficult lesson—one every believer must learn: we can find ourselves in the middle of God's perfect will and in the middle of a perfect storm at the same time!

That day by the Sea of Galilee, God's will couldn't have been clearer to the disciples: Jesus had said, "Let's go!" They didn't call a meeting to deliberate; they didn't pray; they didn't seek counsel from others. God's will had been right there in front of them, so without hesitation, they got into the boat. And now the thing that loomed right in front of them was death.

This unexpected peril was something new for the disciples. So far, following Jesus hadn't been overly costly—little more than quitting their jobs and getting a bit of carping and criticism from local religious leaders (Mark 3:22). But they had faced nothing life threatening. In fact, it had been just the opposite; they were close associates of the most popular person in Galilee. They'd been welcomed in small towns as heroes. This movement of God was working, and all systems were go.

Then came the perfect storm. It certainly raised some questions.

Many people believe faith is some kind of insurance against high blood pressure and heartache. *Trust God and you'll have no worries.* But a great paradox of Christianity is that trusting Christ doesn't keep the storms away. In fact, sometimes it pushes us into deep and turbulent waters.

Jesus faced a perfect storm when He rode into Jerusalem on the back of a donkey. He knew what He was about to face—unthinkable torture and death—and He dreaded it. In the garden He cried out, "O My Father, if it is possible, let this cup pass from Me; nevertheless, not as I will, but as You will" (Matthew 26:39). He was fully aware of the storm He was heading into.

The disciples in their tossing boat weren't cognizant of

these underlying spiritual issues. Fear gripped them, pushing aside all concerns about being in the will of God. But they were about to learn a priceless lesson: there is security in the heart of God's will. Storms are not punishment for lack of obedience; oftentimes they are the *result* of obedience! Those men were in that storm because they had jumped in the boat when Jesus said, "Let's go!"

You will follow Jesus into a storm someday. And you will learn that, although it may be overwhelming, it's the safest of all harbors.

The Presence in the Storms of Our Lives

He was in the stern, asleep on a pillow. And they awoke Him and said to Him, "Teacher, do You not care that we are perishing?"

MARK 4:38

Juan Carlos Ortiz is a well-known preacher, evangelist, and author originally from Argentina. He once related a conversation he had with a circus trapeze artist about the security a safety net provides. The performer said yes, the net does the obvious—it keeps performers from being injured should they fall. But it does much more. "Imagine there is no net," he said. "We would be so nervous that we would be more likely to miss and fall. If there was not a net, we would not dare to do some of the things we do. But because there's a net, we dare to make two turns, and once I made three turns—thanks to the net!"

Ortiz saw an application for Christians: "We have security in God. When we are sure in His arms, we dare to attempt big things for God. We dare to be holy. We dare to be obedient. We dare, because we know the eternal arms of God will hold us if we fall."[2]

The disciples had yet to learn the nature of their "net." If they'd realized the full power and authority Jesus held, they would have laughed and shouted at the wind, "Bring it on!" Facing a storm is exhilarating when we are protected by something even more powerful.

Our degree of fear is a gauge of our degree of faith. When we've trusted Jesus and come through the storm, we become more fearless. If we've never really done that, the storm will reduce us to quivering jelly, as it did those disciples.

Some people do believe in the power of God, but they're not sure about His presence. That's a significant deficiency in one's faith. *Will He really be there when I'm in a crisis? Does He care about me?* We can believe in a powerful God who can create a universe, but if He is absent when needed, how does that belief make a difference? Isn't His absence basically the same as if He didn't exist at all?

This was the crisis the disciples faced. They knew that Jesus was there, but apparently they didn't realize He was God. This meant they were unaware of God's presence. Thus, they didn't know what Jesus could and would do. As I witness the fearful lives of many Christians, I'm convinced that the disciples aren't the only ones in that boat, so to speak.

John Paton was a nineteenth-century Scottish missionary

who labored for a lifetime among murderous natives of the New Hebrides Islands. He often faced danger as various tribesmen sought to kill him. He wrote, "Without that abiding consciousness of the presence and power of my dear Lord and Saviour, nothing else in all the world could have preserved me from losing my reason and perishing miserably."[3]

He said that it was in those most dangerous of moments, when he faced the weapons of men, that he saw the face of Christ most clearly.

On one occasion Paton hid within the branches of a tree as the men below searched for him. He heard their murderous threats, yet he knew he was safe in the arms of Jesus. "Alone, yet not alone!" he recalled. "My comfort and joy sprang from the promise, 'Lo, I am with you always.'"[4]

On the Sea of Galilee, an exhausted Jesus slept on a cushion in the rear of the boat with the waves crashing all about Him. The image is striking. How did the disciples view Him? Apparently, they saw Him as a man much like themselves, even though He possessed the supernatural power to heal the sick and feed the hungry, and—as they would soon find out—the power to calm the wind and the waves.

The Peace in the Storms of Our Lives

He arose and rebuked the wind, and said to the sea, "Peace, be still!" And the wind ceased and there was a great calm.

MARK 4:39

The disciples must have wondered how Jesus could possibly nap with the waves crashing and the wind howling. They shook Him, yelling for Him to wake up: "'Do You not care that we are perishing?' Then He arose and rebuked the wind, and said to the sea, 'Peace, be still!' And the wind ceased and there was a great calm" (Mark 4:38-39). The crisis was at an end. No doubt one could hear the pounding heartbeats of twelve shocked men.

The passage tells us that Jesus rebuked the wind, just as a parent would rebuke an unruly child. He dealt with demons in the same way—He rebuked them (Luke 4:35). And the wind obeyed Him just as demons did. He had power over both the natural and the supernatural.

This enormous display of miraculous power should have quelled any remaining doubts in the minds of the disciples as to who Jesus was. Only God has such authority. The Old Testament tells us that He has power over nature: "He calms the storm, so that its waves are still" (Psalm 107:29; see also Psalm 89:9; 93:4). Before His disciples' eyes, Jesus demonstrated that He possessed power that could emanate only from God. Apparently they hadn't grasped this fact until they saw Him halt a storm in its tracks. Some things must be seen to be believed.

During their three years of following Jesus, these men witnessed ever-greater displays of God's power through Him. They believed, not because they were taught, but because they were shown. The disciples were like newborn spiritual babes whose eyes were slowly opening to the true identity of this Man they followed.

God is committed to developing our spiritual sight as well. And He often uses the storms of life to show us that we can put our hope in Him—His power, love, and wisdom.

Joni Eareckson Tada illustrates how drawing on the power and peace of Jesus transforms her life:

> "O God," I often pray in the morning, "God, I cannot do this. I cannot do this thing called quadriplegia. I have no resources for this. I have no strength for this—but you do. You've got resources. You've got strength. I can't do quadriplegia, but I can do all things through you as you strengthen me [Phil. 4:13]. I have no smile for this woman who's going to walk into my bedroom in a moment. She could be having coffee with another friend, but she's chosen to come here to help me get up. Oh, God, please may I borrow your smile?"[5]

Our loving heavenly Father is kind and patient with us when the storms of life overwhelm us and fill us with anxiety. He is gracious to show us His power even when we are beginning to wonder if He is asleep or absent, even when our cries to Him for help are permeated with doubt. But we can face whatever circumstances await us with courage if we just reflect on God's faithfulness and place our confidence in His great power and loving purpose for our lives.

The Purpose of Storms in Our Lives

Did Jesus bring about this storm simply so He could calm it and build His disciples' faith? The Bible gives no direct answer, but I'm inclined to say no. He had no need to create new storms to demonstrate His true nature, because this fallen world stirs up more than enough trouble on its own. He builds our faith by using the storms that are already there. So I see no reason to believe that Jesus went to sleep for any other purpose than to catch some much-needed rest. Yet He was quick to use the storm as a teachable moment. The storm brought Him their full attention, and the lesson would never be forgotten.

Since you are a human being, I think I'm safe in saying you have no shortage of storms in your life. As someone has said, we're always in one of three places: heading into a storm, in a storm, or emerging from a storm. Because we live in a fallen world, trouble of some kind is woven into the fabric of life. Until these storms hit, we live with "delusions of adequacy," as someone put it. We think we have it all under control—until suddenly we don't. Storms cut us down to size and cause us to fear what we cannot control.

Although God does not create the storms in our life, He does what Jesus did that night on the Sea of Galilee. He uses the churning seas to demonstrate His power and strengthen our faith in Him.

C. S. Lewis explains it like this:

God, who has made us, knows what we are and that our happiness lies in Him. Yet we will not seek it in Him as long as He leaves us any other resort where it can even plausibly be looked for. While what we call "our own life" remains agreeable, we will not surrender it to Him. What then can God do in our interests but make "our own life" less agreeable to us, and take away the plausible source of false happiness?[6]

God knows we need Him, and He knows we forget how much we do. Sometimes He allows the storms to rage so they will send us scurrying to Him, as did those disciples in that tossing boat.

David, the psalmist, discovered the value of the storms God allowed him to go through:

It is good for me that I have been afflicted,
That I may learn Your statutes.
PSALM 119:71

Jesus allowed the winds to rage in order that His disciples would learn to trust Him. Through the storms of life, our Lord teaches us many precious lessons. He reminds us of our own emptiness and our total dependence on Him. He teaches us to fear God with astonished reverence and not to fear the storms.

The Product of Storms in Our Lives

*[Jesus] said to them, "Why are you so fearful? How is it
that you have no faith?" And they feared exceedingly, and
said to one another, "Who can this be, that even the wind
and the sea obey Him!"*

MARK 4:40-41

Jesus was gentler with His disciples than He was with the
wind. While He rebuked the wind, He only asked His disciples two questions: "Why are you so fearful? How is it
that you have no faith?" (Mark 4:40). With these questions,
Jesus reveals a key spiritual truth: the opposite of faith is not
unbelief; the opposite of faith is *fear*. Belief breeds confidence, while unbelief breeds fear. Essentially, Jesus was saying, "Why are you afraid? Do you not yet trust God, whose
power is present in Me?"

The disciples apparently assumed that Jesus was indiffer-
ent to their plight. They cried, "Teacher, do You not care that
we are perishing?" Elijah's suggestion that Baal might have
been asleep is precisely the complaint the disciples leveled at
Jesus: "You're sleeping while we're drowning! Wake up!"

Maybe there's a specific fear claiming your attention
today. Whatever that fear is, it will only be amplified by failure to place our hope in God. He is not sleeping. He is here;
He knows every thought in your mind, every feeling in your
heart. While you stare with apprehension or even terror at
the dark skies, He focuses on the person He is forming you

to be. He sees those storms as growing pains—part of the formation process. He knows that a storm may be the very thing that awakens you to deep faith in Him.

What really intrigues me about this account is that Jesus replaced their fear with *more fear*! After gaping in awe at the suddenly calm and windless sea, "they feared exceedingly, and said to one another, 'Who can this be, that even the wind and the sea obey Him!'" (Mark 4:41). Several Bible translations say, "They were terrified." They suddenly realized they were in the presence of a power they had never imagined— a power residing in a Person mightier than the violence of a stormy sea.

At this point, the disciples were still learning the extraordinary truth the apostle Paul later expressed in Colossians 1:16: "By Him all things were created that are in heaven and that are on earth." It never entered the disciples' heads that Jesus actually *created* the Sea of Galilee, that the winds and waters are *His*. The disciples in that boat-shaped classroom were beginning to recognize that Jesus was greater—and more fearsome—than anything or anyone they could imagine.

The disciples' fear made a critical transition from being self-centered to being Christ-centered. They no longer worried about drowning; now they were in awe of Jesus and felt a new sense of security in Him. Debilitating fears were being replaced with the empowering fear of God, whom they dimly began to realize was present in the Man before them.

Jesus wants us to be overcome with awe and wonder at

His power so we're never deeply frightened again. If He has to use every storm that tears at our sails, He will do it because He's determined to bring us to maturity.

The Promises for the Storms in Our Lives

Before the disciples set out on the Sea of Galilee, Jesus said, "Let us cross over to the other side" (Mark 4:35). If Jesus named a destination, it was certain they would reach it. Could there be a storm? Certainly. Would it be a comfortable voyage? No assurance of that. The disciples could have worried about seasickness, but they didn't need to worry about drowning. Jesus had told them where they were going.

It's really no different for us. From our point of view, the days ahead are uncertain. We don't know their content or their count. But we know our destination. We've been told that Jesus has gone ahead to prepare a place for us (John 14:1-3). The Word of God is filled with such promises, and to grasp them is to have the cure for fear.

God's Word Assures Us of a Safe Landing

Notice what Jesus said to the disciples as they began their journey: "On the same day, when evening had come, He said to them, '*Let us cross over to the other side*'" (Mark 4:35, emphasis added). Now consider what the text says about the end of the journey: "Then they came *to the other side* of the sea, to the country of the Gadarenes" (Mark 5:1, emphasis added).

God's Word assures us of a safe landing: we will make it to the other side. There are two kinds of destinations that deserve our attention: temporary destinations and our ultimate destination. God assures us that we will arrive at our ultimate destination—life in His eternal Kingdom. That promise alone should dispel all manner of fear—fear of storms and the fear of fear itself. If God says that those in Christ will be saved, they will be saved.

But are we guaranteed passage through every storm en route to that ultimate destination? No. Think of all the saints who died as martyrs. I find it significant that, once death was certain, many of these heroes of the faith died without fear. They could do so only because they had complete faith in God's assurance of their ultimate destination.

Could you die like that? If your day were today, would you feel the joy of knowing you were going to reach the farther shore? In Christ, death loses all power to terrify.

God's Word Alerts Us to Expect Stormy Seas

I find it illuminating that the apostle James, the half brother of Jesus, used the metaphor of a stormy sea when he talked about trials (James 1:2-8). He says we will encounter storms in this life, and without faith we will be "like a wave of the sea driven and tossed by the wind" (James 1:6).

"My brethren," James writes, "count it all joy *when* you fall into various trials" (verse 2, emphasis added). Note that he doesn't say *if* but *when*. Clear skies are never promised in the Bible, though some struggle to embrace that idea. Even Jesus, who lived a perfect life, was given no exemption from storms. Hebrews 5:8 tells us that He was allowed to suffer, and Romans 8:32 explains why, telling us that God "did not spare His own Son, but delivered Him up for us all." God allowed His Son to suffer so that we might be spared the punishment we've earned and go on to enjoy every good gift God gives us.

If Jesus had to suffer, why would we think ourselves exempt? After all, as He explained, "a disciple is not above his teacher, nor a servant above his master" (Matthew 10:24). Then He told them not to fear the storms that inevitably would assail them (verse 26).

Jesus gives us the key to surviving storms in His story about two houses: one built on the sand, the other on solid rock. The sand represents the shallow, shifting, and unreliable values of worldly culture. The rock represents the unshakable truth of God (Matthew 7:24-27). As the storm rages, the first house quickly topples into the sand and washes out to sea. The other stands firm, withstanding the force of the most violent winds. In decades of ministry, I have often seen the truth of this parable vividly demonstrated. People who place their hope in God withstand every storm because they have built their lives on the only foundation that cannot be moved.

God's Word Announces That the Savior Is on Board

The disciples were too inexperienced with Jesus to have a faith devoid of fear. Perhaps you're the same way. You identify with Christ, but you draw no assurance as the clouds roll in. When the sky darkens, you might wonder whether you should step into the boat with Jesus or stay ashore in hopes of avoiding the storm. The problem with that choice is that it's a false one. You can run, but you cannot hide. The storms will find you. You don't get to decide whether the rain is coming; you only get to decide whether to carry an umbrella.

"But He is sleeping," you say. "He doesn't care." Don't let His seeming silence lead you to conclude that He isn't with you. He says, "I will never leave you nor forsake you" (Hebrews 13:5). As He told His disciples, "Lo, I am with you always, even to the end of the age" (Matthew 28:20).

Those are promises, and He has yet to break a promise. That He will be with you is the most certain fact of your life. What's uncertain is your grasp of that fact—your ability to trust and to build your house upon that truth. It's the only storm-proof foundation in existence.

Adoniram Judson was America's first foreign missionary. He devoted his life to God's service, and yet he lost his wife and then, three months later, their infant daughter, Maria. Judson was overcome with grief. He had been away, doing his Father's business, during his wife's illness, and he found it nearly impossible to forgive himself. He wrote, "God is to me the great Unknown. I believe in him but I find him not."[7]

In spite of this anguished expression of aloneness, Judson didn't lose his faith. Sometimes the rains pound hard enough to drown out all other voices, and we struggle to hear Christ calming the storm. But that doesn't mean He isn't calming it.

The storms pass, and we hear the voice of God once again—
this time through a new wisdom tempered by our struggles.
And we realize that He was there all the time.

> God is our refuge and strength,
> A very present help in trouble.
> Therefore we will not fear,
> Even though the earth be removed,
> And though the mountains be carried into the midst of
>   the sea;
> Though its waters roar and be troubled,
> Though the mountains shake with its swelling.
>
> PSALM 46:1-3

God's Word Affirms That Faith Drives Out Fear

Charles Spurgeon uses two biblical examples to show how
one's faith can grow to be stronger and more complete. The
first is David, who says, "Whenever I am afraid, I will trust in
You" (Psalm 56:3). The second example is Isaiah, who says,
"I will trust and not be afraid" (Isaiah 12:2).

Charles Spurgeon compares the faith of these two men
to medicines, with Isaiah's being the stronger brand. He
tells about a man who got the chills but gave thanks for the
prescription that helped him through them. A neighbor
said, "Thankful for that? I have something that would keep
you from getting the chills in the first place!" If you have
a faith that helps you deal with fear, said Spurgeon, good

for you. But why not go after a higher-grade faith that is fear resistant?[8]

When the disciples stepped into the boat with Jesus, they did not even have the first kind of faith. They didn't put their hope in Jesus, so their fear escalated to sheer terror. When Jesus awoke and calmed the storm, the dawning realization of who He really was ratcheted their faith to a new level. Later we learn that they became utterly fearless, proclaiming the truth of the Kingdom in the face of all kinds of storms. Had they possessed mature faith that day in the boat, they could have curled up and napped with Jesus with no regard for the storm raging about them.

No matter what your trouble is, you can call on God in the midst of it, and He will calm the storm. But deep is the joy of the one who calls on God *before* the storm, for he will find that his faith drives out all fear.

CHAPTER 2

HOPE AFTER FAILURE

The LORD, He is the One who goes before you.
He will be with you, He will not leave you nor forsake you;
do not fear nor be dismayed.

DEUTERONOMY 31:8

Lyndon Baines Johnson was ambitious from the start. He moved smoothly through the House of Representatives, was elected to the Senate, and then became the Senate's majority leader. Still, his eyes never left one address: 1600 Pennsylvania Avenue—the White House.

He was a tall Texan—six foot four—not to mention wealthy and influential. He had a reputation for getting things done, even if he had to cut a few corners along the way. By the end of a typical day, he had outworked and out-maneuvered everyone in the room. He wouldn't take no for an answer on anything, including his drive to be president of the United States.

In the two years leading up to the 1960 campaign, it seemed like his greatest dream lay within his grip. He was the highest-ranking Democrat in the nation and one of the most respected men in America. His opponent was considered a lightweight in politics—a skinny, sickly young man who, in Johnson's view, was little more than a playboy living on his father's money: John F. Kennedy.

Summoning advisers to his Texas ranch in 1958, Johnson told them plainly that it was his destiny to be president and that he was going to run for the office.

So the men around him began to lay the foundation for a campaign to put their man in the White House. Since the Republicans had held the presidency for two terms, the Democrats poured all they had into their leading light. The planners waited for Johnson's announcement that he would throw his ten-gallon hat in the ring.

Then they waited some more.

Johnson, who had spoken of this dream for as long as anyone had known him, had cold feet. He was, according to the White House press secretary at the time, "a man badly torn."[1] Meanwhile, Kennedy was racing across the nation sewing up delegates to win the nomination for himself. By the time Johnson got around to announcing his candidacy, it was too late. Kennedy had beaten him to the punch.

Historians have speculated why such a driven and powerful man stalled at the most important moment of his career. Biographer Robert A. Caro has a theory. He believes that for all his drive and bravado, Johnson was paralyzed by a fear of failure—the fear that he would end up like his father.

When Lyndon was a child, his family was among the most respected in town, living in a large house on a sprawling Texas ranch. His father, Samuel, was a successful man—a member of the state House and the most prosperous businessman in the area. Sam bought the first car anyone had ever seen in those parts, and he had a chauffeur to drive it. The Johnson family was riding high.

But just as young Lyndon came into his teenage years, disaster struck: the business failed. The family lost its ranch and moved into a little shanty house, the next step up from homelessness. From being the highest in society, the Johnsons plummeted to the lowest. Townspeople brought food to keep them from starving. Lyndon was humiliated beyond words. One classmate recalls that when Lyndon was taunted at school, he responded that one day he would be president of the United States. His classmates laughed and said they wouldn't vote for him. He retorted that he wouldn't need their votes.

From that moment, LBJ dreamed of being president. But when the prize was finally within his grasp, he was traumatized by a fear of failing in a way that would bring public humiliation, as had happened to his father. He was so afraid of defeat that it became a self-fulfilling prophecy.

Caro writes,

> His father's fall had shown him that failure could mean not merely failure but terror, the terror of

living in a house that, month by month, you were afraid would be taken from you by the bank; that failure could mean not merely terror but ruin, permanent ruin; that failure—defeat—might be something from which you would never recover. And failure in public—failing in a way that was visible: having to move off your ranch; having your credit cut off at stores you had to walk past every day; no longer holding your public office—could mean a different, but also terrible, kind of pain: embarrassment, disgrace, humiliation.[2]

According to Caro, that's why Johnson anguished and languished over his run for office. And that's why Kennedy beat him for the 1960 nomination and history took the strange and twisted course that followed. He did eventually make it to 1600 Pennsylvania Avenue, but it wasn't by a course he ever would have scripted out for himself.

Those who fear failure are paralyzed by the "*r* word": *risk*. They may undermine their own efforts without even realizing it in an attempt to escape the anxiety of looming failure. Have you known people like that? I have—gifted people who might have done great things in life but wouldn't, and couldn't, because they were protecting themselves from disappointment.

Nearly all of us have felt the fear of failure at some point in our lives. In fact, many of the most-admired people in the Bible experienced it. We see this consistently in the "call narratives" of the Bible—those accounts in which God summons a person to a particular task. The more prominent examples are Moses, Gideon, Isaiah, Jeremiah, and Ezekiel.

In the Old Testament, these call narratives have a similar form and progression. First there is an encounter with God, either directly or through one of His angels. This encounter occurs not in some sacred place but within the normal routines of life. Moses is tending sheep, and Gideon is threshing wheat. A divine encounter ensues, bringing a call and challenge: *Your moment has arrived—I am sending you on the mission of your life!*

The calling is usually followed by objections from the person called—many of them born out of a fear of failure. Moses responded to his call by saying: "Who am I that I should go to Pharaoh, and that I should bring the children of Israel out of Egypt?" (Exodus 3:11). Even after God's assurances of success, Moses continued to object: "O my Lord, I am not eloquent . . . but I am slow of speech and slow of tongue" (Exodus 4:10).

When God called Gideon to fight against the Midianites, his initial response was similar: "O my Lord, how can I save Israel? Indeed my clan is the weakest in Manasseh, and I am the least in my father's house" (Judges 6:15). When God called Jeremiah to speak words of prophecy to God's people, Jeremiah's objection follows the same pattern: "Then said I: 'Ah, Lord God! Behold, I cannot speak, for I am a youth'" (Jeremiah 1:6).

Obviously, the fear of failure is not a modern phenomenon;

it is a timeless human fear. Some of God's choicest servants through the ages displayed this fear in spite of God's promises of success. Their stories provide insight into how God responds to human fears. In every case, He draws alongside His servant with assurance and affirmation.

Nowhere is God's concern for a fearful servant more evident than in Joshua 1, where He prepares Joshua to lead Israel after the death of Moses. In this chapter, I will focus mainly on this call and its accompanying assurance, because here all the principles scattered throughout the other call narratives come together in an organized, step-by-step strategy for dealing with the fear of failure. The theme of Joshua's call is transition—the transition of Israel's leadership from Moses to Joshua. To fully appreciate the magnitude of this transition, we must remember the greatness of Moses.

He is certainly the most revered figure in Judaism, and he ranks among the greatest men in history. An entire generation of Israelites followed Moses out of slavery and into the wilderness. Deuteronomy 34 tells how he died at the ripe age of 120, still a sharp and vigorous man. Israel had seen no other prophet of Moses' caliber—a man so close to God, so endowed with God's miraculous power. They had seen him raise his staff as God parted the waters of the Red Sea. They had seen him stand up to Pharaoh and call down bread from heaven. They had waited at the base of the mountain as God dictated His Ten Commandments to him.

The book of Exodus makes a statement about Moses that is not said of any other person in Scripture: "The LORD spoke to Moses face to face, as a man speaks to his friend" (Exodus 33:11). On more than one occasion, Moses even spent forty days on a mountain in fellowship with Him. God grants this kind of intimacy only to those who desire it. Moses belonged to an inner circle of people who enjoyed holy intimacy with God.

The people would grumble against Moses, but in the end they would always follow him, for they knew he was God's man. His leadership filled them with frustration at first, then deeper devotion. And when the great man finally died, they wept in the plains of Moab for thirty days (Deuteronomy 34:8).

There's no question—Moses would have been a hard act to follow. That was the call to greatness that thrust itself upon Joshua.

Moses' death came at a perilous time in Israel's history. The previous generation had been too fearful to put their hope in God's promise of victory and refused to enter the Promised Land at its very border (Numbers 13–14). That entire generation had died off during thirty-eight years of wandering in the wilderness. Now an all-new generation was gathered on the east bank of the Jordan River, ready to cross over and take possession of the Promised Land. They were ready to step out in faith and claim their home. But it wasn't going to be easy—it never is.

For one thing, after four decades of peace, the Israelites

hadn't fought a serious battle for forty years, and the Canaanites they would soon face were said to be tall, sturdy, battle-hardened warriors who made the Israelite spies feel "like grasshoppers" in comparison (Numbers 13:33). The enemy waited behind strong, fortified walls. They even had horses and chariots (Joshua 17:16).

Then there was the problem of food. The people had grown accustomed to receiving manna from the hand of God at their doorstep each morning. Now, as we read in Exodus 16:35 and Joshua 5:12, the manna would cease, and the Israelites would be responsible for cultivating food from the land.

How would you like to have been Joshua, taking the reins of leadership from someone like Moses at such a critical time? If you had been called in as a consultant to help Joshua prepare for his new role, what would your counsel have been? Actually, Joshua did have a consultant—God Himself. God delivered to Joshua one of the greatest motivational speeches I've ever read. His words have often encouraged me at times of great personal challenge.

If you are afraid about your future, if you are being called to a new assignment that seems beyond your abilities, or if you just need encouragement to continue on in whatever God has called you to do, you, too, will find courage as you study God's charge to Joshua in the face of his greatest challenge. We'll explore six powerful principles from Joshua to send you forth as a conqueror rather than a hostage to your own fear of failure.

The Principle of Divine Perspective

As I was with Moses, so I will be with you. I will not leave you nor forsake you.

JOSHUA 1:5

God looked upon an anxious new leader and gave him the words of a lifetime. He began by reminding Joshua of the adventures he had enjoyed as Moses' protégé through the years. Joshua had been witness to a rich history of miracles and magnificence, of God proving His faithfulness in a trek through a hostile empire and then into the wilderness.

God encouraged Joshua to remember what he had experienced as Moses' partner in ministry—how He had led Moses and how He had performed mighty acts to help Moses lead the people. God assured Joshua, "As I was with Moses, so I will be with you." Joshua was to view his daunting task through the perspective of God's previous demonstrations of power and faithfulness.

I love to read biographies of Christian leaders because they remind me of the principle of divine perspective. As God has been faithful to His followers in the past, He will be faithful to us in the present. He has put no limits on what He is willing to do for you and me. His actions might even exceed what He has done in the past. He is able "to do exceedingly abundantly above all that we ask or think" (Ephesians 3:20).

Fear of failure is nothing new—nor is overcoming it.

Think of the seventeenth-century Pilgrims who left their homes to find freedom of worship in the New World. They must have been daunted by the prospect of crossing the Atlantic in their tiny ships and surviving in an uncharted wilderness. But they overcame their fear because they had faith in God's power and provision. That is the benefit of perspective—it allows us to see beyond the trials that frighten us in the here and now.

God has never called anyone to a task and then abandoned him or her by the side of the road. So if we fear what God wants us to do, our perspective needs adjusting so that we focus not on the size of the job but on the size of God.

The Principle of Divine Purpose

Arise, go over this Jordan, you and all this people, to the land which I am giving to them—the children of Israel. Every place that the sole of your foot will tread upon I have given you, as I said to Moses.

JOSHUA 1:2-3

God gave Joshua a specific thing to do! He told Joshua to walk on every piece of ground in the land of Canaan and promised him that every piece of ground he walked on would be given to him and to his people forever. God was giving Joshua *focus*.

The 1993 movie *The Fugitive*, starring Harrison Ford, was nominated for seven Academy Awards, winning one.

It grossed nearly $369 million worldwide. But the movie almost didn't get made. The script was in development for five and a half years. Nine different writers produced at least twenty-five different screenplays. Producer Arnold Kopelson said,

> There were times that everyone would say, "You're wasting your time. Why are you doing this? You're wasting money." Warner Brothers put the property into turn-around. . . . We had spent about two million dollars in writing costs and they were concerned that this would never bear out. And I said, "Listen, I have an instinct about this. My gut tells me that this is going to be a success."[3]

Granted, sometimes instincts and gut feelings don't work out. But in this case, they did. Kopelson's determination illustrates an important point: maintaining purpose and focus in the face of obstacles can be the difference between failure and success.

Seeing *The Fugitive* through to opening day meant the producer had to stay focused for more than five years. But Joshua had to maintain his own focus for fourteen years, the time required to win the Promised Land. It helped that Joshua didn't have to trust his gut feeling; he had the promises of God.

J. Oswald Sanders helps us understand this promise to Joshua:

The land belonged to Israel by direct gift from God, Possessor of heaven and earth. The land became theirs experientially only when they walked around it and actually took possession. This fundamental spiritual principle carries over into the experience of the New Testament Christian. "According to your faith let it be to you" (Matthew 9:29).[4]

But having a promise from God is no guarantee of success if we lose our focus. God's responsibility is to make the promise; ours is to stay focused on it in the face of fear. To achieve success, Joshua and the new generation of Israelites had to focus their minds and hearts on the purpose God had given them.

There's a special, liberating power in knowing exactly what it is we must do. That's why people derive great satisfaction from making and checking off to-do lists. To boil down all the complexities of the day into bullet points of activity is to see our way to productivity. On the other hand, whole organizations fail because people are confused about their job descriptions. Set a clear focus in your life, and fear will be crowded out. The more you fix your hope on God's purpose for you, the more you will overcome your fear.

The Principle of Divine Persuasion

Have I not commanded you? Be strong and of good courage.
JOSHUA 1:9

While Reverend William Sykes was the chaplain of University College, Oxford, he described a group of undergraduates with physical disabilities he had known. Their limitations were many, but what linked them together was a quiet courage within them. This experience caused him to ponder the meaning of that word. Looking to the writings of Cardinal Manning, he found this entry:

> The Italians call it *Coraggio*, or greatness of heart; the Spaniards, *Corage*[*sic*]; the French, *Courage*, from whom we have borrowed it. And we understand it to mean manliness, bravery, boldness, fearlessness, springing not from a sense of physical power, or from insensibility to danger or pain, but from the moral habit of self-command, with deliberation, fully weighing present dangers, and clearly foreseeing future consequences, and yet in the path of duty advancing unmoved to its execution.[5]

Somehow, the students had found a strength inside that transcended their physical limitations. Faith is an inestimable power, and often it grows by the convincing words of someone who persuades us that we, too, can live courageously.

Who among us does not have some kind of disability—in skill, desire, motivation, strength, experience, courage, or the countless other traits required to make good progress in life? It's called being human—and it's why every person needs the same exhortation Joshua needed when he stood on the banks of the Jordan River and looked across to a hostile land.

He must have remembered what happened when the Israelites stood at the borders of the Promised Land almost forty years earlier. They had God's promise, yet the challenge paralyzed them. It wasn't the giants in the land that disabled them; it was their giant fear. To prevent this new generation from making the same mistake, Joshua needed to display strength and courage. This meant he needed to be persuaded that God would enable them to meet the challenge. God had just the right words for Israel's new leader:

> *Be strong and of good courage. . . . Only be strong and*
> *very courageous. . . . Have I not commanded you? Be*
> *strong and of good courage.*
>
> JOSHUA 1:6-7, 9

This is the heart of God's motivational speech to Joshua. Three times He tells him to be strong and courageous. The word *strong* means to be resolute, firm, and not easily swayed. *Courageous* conveys a sense of daring, an openness to risk.

Joshua had proved that he had that inner strength within him. We witness it on the day the spies returned, ten of them giving a fearful report of unconquerable giants. Only two men, Joshua and Caleb, wanted to take hold of God's promises and push forward despite the obstacles. The ten insisted, "We are not able to go up against the people, for they are stronger than we" (Numbers 13:31). The tales of terror drowned out the counsel of courage.

When we face such a situation, we'll either focus on the problem or on the solution. Ten men turned into grasshoppers in their own eyes simply by giving rein to their fear; two men focused on God and His power. Ten spoke of the size of the enemy; two spoke of the size of their God.

Sometimes the majority gets it wrong. The wisdom of God is often found on the narrow path that few travel rather than in the easy and popular choice. Leadership is a great deal more than gauging which way the wind is blowing. It often requires standing firm as the current tries to bend you in another direction.

Paul Laurence Dunbar's little poem makes this point:

Minorities, since time began,
Have shown the better side of man;
And often in the lists of Time
One man has made a cause sublime![6]

When I've faced challenges in my life, I've drawn inspiration from envisioning Joshua at the banks of his river, learning to be strong and courageous, or holding on to the words of Paul: "If God is for us, who can be against us?" (Romans 8:31). These inspiring passages persuade me to be firm and willing to take risks for God. I believe this practice will work for you as well.

The Principle of Divine Priority

Do not turn from it to the right hand or to the left, that
you may prosper wherever you go. This Book of the Law
shall not depart from your mouth, but you shall meditate
in it day and night, that you may observe to do according
to all that is written in it.

JOSHUA 1:7-8

Now we come to the heart of the matter: God's Word is the only path to success.

God didn't tell Joshua that his priority needed to be military strategy, financial backing, or bilateral relations with neighboring countries. These things have a place, but they are not the priority. Here was Joshua's priority: meditate day and night on the principles of the Word of God.

This requires dedication somewhat like that of a long-distance runner who is training to compete in an Olympic marathon. The runners I've read about are incredibly focused. They live with a Spartan's commitment to a single priority— winning that marathon and standing on an Olympic podium. Running informs every aspect of their lives. They eat specific foods, weighing the grams and counting the calories. They monitor their weight, body fat, water weight, and bone density. They run in only a certain kind of shoe. They have limited social lives because running, training, eating, and sleeping dominate their days. Their training schedule is the paradigm into which all of life's activities fit. Their conversations and their daily decisions reflect their mission. When planning and executing their lives, everything flows through the grid of training.

When asked what he would be doing if he weren't a runner, one marathoner from Kenya laughed and said, "I don't know. For me, running is everything." I urge you to read the following five points about Scripture with that perspective so you can say, "For me, the Word of God is everything. It informs all my decisions and values. I arrange my life around its principles. I study it consistently to reinforce my life goals. I consult it before I make plans or decisions. What the Bible says takes precedence over whatever anyone else says. It is, after all, *God's* Word."

Scripture is my weapon of choice in the fight against the fear of defeat. As we seek courage to conquer the giants in our lives, we need to make our top priority the Word of God.

Talk about the Word Constantly

This Book of the Law shall not depart from your mouth.
JOSHUA 1:8

Let's clarify what Joshua would have understood to be the "Book of the Law." For him it was the first five books of our Bible—the Pentateuch, as that collection of books is called. Nothing more of Scripture had yet been written. God told Joshua that this book was to be his plan of action. He was to take this book in his hands and commit it to his heart. It was the key to his ability to accomplish the assignment God was giving him.

The Book of the Law was also to be the topic of his conversation with others—not talking about it as we would a novel or a biography, but allowing the law of God to inform, guide, and temper all conversations and deliberations. Later in the book, we see Joshua doing that very thing:

> *Afterward he read all the words of the law, the blessings and the cursings, according to all that is written in the Book of the Law. There was not a word of all that Moses had commanded which Joshua did not read before all the assembly of Israel.*
>
> JOSHUA 8:34-35

Part of what Joshua would have read to the people was the passage in Deuteronomy 6:6-9, Moses' instructions to parents about how to weave the Word of God into their children's lives: "You . . . shall talk of [God's words] when you sit in your house, when you walk by the way, when you lie down, and when you rise up" (verse 7).

Notice the word *talk*. God's words, commands, and statutes—His perspective on everything—were to be embedded in every family conversation. Children would grow up with God's law deeply entrenched in their very thinking.

The Deuteronomy passage also uses a figure of speech that involves making a point by giving opposites: when you're in the house, when you're outside; when you're lying down, when you're up and about; when you're sitting, when you're standing. The idea is that we teach the law all the time—now, then, and every moment in between.

God's law should live on the tongue. There is no inappropriate time for sharing it, and we should be as driven to discuss it as a bird is to sing. The Lord provides all the various venues of life—relaxed family time, outdoor chores, coming-of-age milestones—for discussing the law in every context. Think what would happen today if Christians, instead of discussing politics, TV shows, movies, sports, and traffic, started talking more about the Word of God!

"What did you learn from the Word today?"

"Before we discuss our plans, let's see what counsel we can find in the Bible."

Wouldn't that be a refreshing way to live? Wouldn't it be a powerful step in putting our hope in Christ and conquering our fears and failings?

Meditate on the Word Continually

You shall meditate in it day and night.
JOSHUA 1:8

The very idea of meditation seems countercultural. We don't like anything slow or deliberate, and we particularly hate the idea of quiet. We like things to be fast paced. We like more action and less reflection. We like 140-character tweets instead of in-depth information.

But meditation—biblical meditation, not the emptying

of the mind featured in Eastern religions—is central to the life to which God calls us. It requires that we give up our hurry and listen quietly and deeply to what God has to say. J. I. Packer describes the right way to do it:

> Meditation is the activity of calling to mind, and thinking over, and dwelling on, and applying to oneself, the various things that one knows about the works and ways and purposes and promises of God.
> Its purpose is to . . . let his truth make its full and proper impact on one's mind and heart. . . . It is, indeed, often a matter of arguing with oneself, reasoning oneself out of moods of doubt and unbelief into a clear apprehension of God's power and grace.[7]

Like a cow that chews the same grass over and over to digest it and benefit from it, we meditate on the Word of God by going over and over it in a way that allows God to speak to our hearts and quiet our fears.

Meditation is preventive maintenance for the mind. We fill every corner of our thinking with rich, eternal truth before the errors of the world can take root there and infect us. We live in this world, and we'll be exposed to all that is wrong about it. But we can make ourselves resistant to the virus of false ideas. Meditating on God's Word is inoculation against "every wind of doctrine" (Ephesians 4:14).

David understood the power of meditation. He wrote,

Oh, how I love Your law!
It is my meditation all the day.
You, through Your commandments, make me wiser
        than my enemies;
For they are ever with me.
I have more understanding than all my teachers,
For Your testimonies are my meditation.
I understand more than the ancients,
Because I keep Your precepts.
PSALM 119:97-100

Try meditating each day on Philippians 4:13, which reads, "I can do all things through Christ who strengthens me." Think about how much more resistant you'd be to the insidious whispers that say, *Give up—you can't do this; God isn't going to help you.* The implanted Word is a bulwark against the lies of the evil one.

Whichever of those two messages touches your soul most frequently—the voice of courage or the voice of defeat—that's the one that wins the battle for your mind.

Read the Word Obediently

. . . that you may observe to do according to all that is
written in [the Book of the Law].
JOSHUA 1:8

Notice the phrase *observe to do* in this passage. It's easy to pass over these three words as negligible, but in reality they present one of the great concepts of the Old Testament. We are not to read the Bible for information only or just to increase our knowledge. We are to study the Bible to discover God's will for our lives. We *observe* in order to *do*. We observe the Bible in order to obey the Bible.

One of the most subtle and dangerous errors we can fall into is to view the Bible simply as interesting reading. Yes, it's timeless literature—fascinating, entertaining, and moving. But at all times the Word of God is no mere book. It's meant to change who we are and how we live. The Bible's message can't simply stop with the mind; it must go on to the heart and the will. We are to be "doers of the word, and not hearers only" (James 1:22).

When we fear living counterculturally as God's light in the world, obedience is the single key to banishing the fear. Disobey, and fear remains. Obey, and fear departs. The role of the Word of God is to tell us what to do. But courage is only realized when we obey.

Follow the Word Exclusively

> Do not turn from [the Book of the Law] to the right hand or to the left.
> JOSHUA 1:7

The phrase *zero tolerance* entered our common language after 1994 legislation outlawed bringing firearms to school. There would be no tolerance for a violation of that decree. Expulsion for one year would follow, and if the school failed to comply, it could lose its federal funding. Zero tolerance meant a strict, clear-cut policy banning guns in schools. The phrase caught on, and soon we were discussing other areas that deserved zero tolerance: bullying, cheating, dealing drugs.

The term didn't exist in Joshua's day, but as the passage above shows, its application did. God gave Joshua a zero-tolerance policy concerning spiritual infidelity, telling him that when Israel entered Canaan, he was to follow the Word of God without turning "to the right hand or to the left."

He wasn't to compromise morality or principles to conform to the practices of the land's inhabitants. He wasn't to massage the meaning of God's law to make it politically correct. He wasn't to use it as a proof text for his own point of view. He was to obey God's law and nothing else.

At the heart of the law was the covenant, the agreement between God and His people. It would not change; a new generation must hold to old revelation. In a time of uncertainty, facing a new world, this would be their assurance: *Nothing important has changed. I, the Lord, do not change. Keep following Me.*

We know the history that followed. The people of Israel took many steps to the left and to the right. God was patient and forgiving, but finally the nation had to suffer for its lack of faithfulness to God and His law. The nation split in two. Its people were exiled first to Assyria, then to Babylon. The Israelites paid the price, living in constant fear of enemies and invasions. They turned to the right hand and the left to serve other gods, and eventually their fears were realized when God removed His umbrella of protection.

We have a choice: we can follow the gods of this world and live with the fear that we'll be caught in the outcomes that inevitably fall on all disobedience, or we can follow God and His Word exclusively and live without fear.

Accept the Word Totally

> . . . *all that is written in it.*
> JOSHUA 1:8

Sometimes people ask me why I preach from the Old Testament. Nearly everyone likes the Gospels of Jesus and the letters of the apostles. But why worry about all those wars and kings and prophets?

There is good reason. I include the Old Testament in my teaching because God's message is incomplete without it. Theology recognizes two kinds of inspiration of Scripture: verbal inspiration means that the words were inspired by God; plenary or full inspiration means that *all* of the Bible comes directly from God. We believe, then, that every word of the Scriptures has God as its source. This is reflected in Joshua 1:8, where the word *all* takes center stage. We aren't to pick and choose from God's law any more than we are to pick and choose what federal laws we obey.

Did Joshua listen? Many years later, when he was nearing death, he gave his final address to the people of Israel, now established in the Promised Land. He echoed the words that were given to him many years earlier by God: "Be very courageous to keep and to do all that is written in the Book of the Law of Moses, lest you turn aside from it to the right hand or to the left" (Joshua 23:6).

In Deuteronomy 17:18-19, God made deep immersion in His law the first priority for Israel's future kings. No doubt this is why David, nearing the end of his life, prepared his son Solomon for accession to kingship with words that echoed God's charge to Joshua:

> I go the way of all the earth; be strong, therefore, and
> prove yourself a man. And keep the charge of the LORD
> your God: to walk in His ways, to keep His statutes, His
> commandments, His judgments, and His testimonies,
> as it is written in the Law of Moses, that you may prosper
> in all that you do and wherever you turn.
>
> 1 KINGS 2:2-3

It is no small thing that God called Joshua to the Word as he stood on the banks of the Jordan. Those who desire to do anything for God and experience the richness He desires for them must be people of the Word.

The "spiritual greats" of our times have made the Word a first priority. Some pastors, leaders, teachers, and laymen have read through the Bible more than a hundred times. It is said that George Müller read it two hundred times. Missionary David Livingston read it four times in succession while he was detained in a jungle town. Charles Spurgeon said, "A Bible that is falling apart usually belongs to someone who is not."

The Bible is the greatest source of encouragement available today. When we read it, we are changed because it is a living book. Whenever we are afraid of failure or feel as if we are failures, the Word of God should be our highest priority. The words we find there will infuse our hearts and minds with strength and courage. The more we focus on God and His Word, the less room there will be for fear.

The Principle of Divine Presence

I will be with you. I will not leave you nor forsake you. . . .
The LORD your God is with you wherever you go.
JOSHUA 1:5, 9

Earlier in this chapter, we discussed the similarities in the call narratives of the Old Testament—the challenge from heaven, the fear from earth, the reaffirmation and assurance from God. There's one other key element: God's consistent promise to accompany us on the journey. He never says, "You go, and I'll wait here for you." He says, "Let's go."

- God said to Moses: "I will certainly be with you. . . . Now therefore, go, and I will be with your mouth and teach you what you shall say" (Exodus 3:12; 4:12).
- To Gideon: "Surely I will be with you, and you shall defeat the Midianites as one man" (Judges 6:16).

- To Jeremiah: "'Do not be afraid of their faces, for I am with you to deliver you,' says the LORD. . . . 'For I am with you,' says the LORD, 'to deliver you'" (Jeremiah 1:8, 19).
- And to Joshua: "As I was with Moses, so I will be with you. I will not leave you nor forsake you" (Joshua 1:5).

For forty years, Joshua had witnessed God's faithful presence with his mentor, Moses. Now God promised Joshua that he, too, would be blessed by the presence of God in his life and leadership.

Nothing is more important, or more confidence boosting, in the call of God than the promise that God will be with us. God's promise of His active presence and power always accompanies every person He calls. This renders meaningless any excuse or objection to the call. Whether the person called feels inadequate or incapable becomes irrelevant, because he carries with him God's power to accomplish what God calls him to do.

In the New Testament, God makes the same promise to us that He made to His Old Testament saints:

"I will never leave you nor forsake you." So we may boldly say:

"The LORD is my helper;
I will not fear.
What can man do to me?"
HEBREWS 13:5-6

The Principle of Divine Prosperity

You will make your way prosperous, and then you will have good success.

JOSHUA 1:8

This is undoubtedly one of the boldest promises in the entire Bible. To most people today, success means the accomplishment of goals and financial achievement. In the Hebrew language, however, it means to be prudent or to act circumspectly. In a spiritual sense, this means letting one's life be guided by God. Joshua had this kind of success and prosperity. He ran into his share of bumps in the road, and he had his failures. But the great scope of his life indicated prudence and wisdom, and he was a successful man.

Now picture this with me: Joshua learns that his new job assignment is to lead these nomadic people against the Canaanites. It's a great promotion, but he fears it's too much for him. Filled with anxiety, he goes into the Divine Consultant's office, where he is given these six principles to overcome his fear of failure and guarantee his success. He walks out standing straight and tall, with a confident spring in his step. He has received a transfusion of courage.

As Joshua came to the end of his life, he gave testimony to the power of these principles to bring prosperity and success to his nation:

Behold, this day I am going the way of all the earth. And
you know in all your hearts and in all your souls that
not one thing has failed of all the good things which the
LORD your God spoke concerning you. All have come to
pass for you; not one word of them has failed.

JOSHUA 23:14

I know these principles work, because I have made them
the core principles for my own walk with God. On many
occasions when I've faced the challenges of ministry, these
powerful words have given me the shot of courage I needed
to push on and find the success God promises. As I write
this chapter, I am reminded of the times when I was most
afraid of failure. The first was my last year in seminary. I had
spent four years in college and four years in graduate seminary training, and within weeks I would have to step out of
that comfort zone into the real world. I remember thinking,
I wonder if I'll be able to do this. What if I'm just not cut out
for the ministry?

My first assignment after graduating was to serve as a
youth pastor and Christian education director at a large
church in New Jersey. Those were great days for Donna and
me. We hung out with the high school kids day and night,
and God gave us the privilege of mentoring some of the
greatest young people we had ever met. We still hear from
some of them to this day.

During the last months of our second year in New Jersey,
I began to feel a growing desire to preach. My few preaching

opportunities made me eager to do more. We didn't have to wait long for that desire to be met. A longtime pastor friend was building a network of churches in Fort Wayne, Indiana. Out of the blue, he called me to ask if I would have any interest in becoming the pastor of their newest church plant.

With many reservations, Donna and I agreed to visit the church. I would preach in the mother church and then meet with the seven families who had agreed to help start this new work. I was pretty certain that God did not want me to do this, but I felt obligated to listen to their proposal.

As we traveled home afterward, we were both overwhelmed with the faith and excitement of this core group of people. And we were shocked that they wanted us to come to lead them in this venture of faith. They gave us a couple of weeks to make our decision, and we ended up taking every single day! As the deadline drew near, I was conflicted. Looking back, I now realize that a big part of my indecision was the fear that I would not be able to accomplish what they wanted me to do. What if we went to Indiana and failed to make the new church a success?

Other issues also clouded my mind. During our visit, I had driven around the area where this church was to be planted, and I counted at least five well-established churches. And I was to be the pastor of seven families meeting in a mobile home! That's right—a mobile home. One of the core members of the new church sold mobile homes, and he had agreed to assemble four of them into an L-shaped arrangement that resulted in an "auditorium" that would seat one hundred people, with the other section housing a nursery, a few classrooms, and a small office.

If you were driving around Fort Wayne, Indiana, looking for a new church home, would you have chosen the mobile home church over one of the five beautiful churches in our part of town? Neither would I! The fear of failure was palpable, and I knew how to get rid of it—stay right where we were in an established, comfortable church.

With only a few days left before the deadline, I drove to the New Jersey shore to spend the day thinking and praying. It was colder than I'd anticipated, so I popped into a coffee shop on the boardwalk to get warm. I took my coffee and a copy of the *Philadelphia Inquirer* to a booth and settled in—and began reading a story that changed our lives.

It was an article about Vince Lombardi, the fabled coach of the Green Bay Packers. He had just left Wisconsin to become head coach of the struggling Washington Redskins. It was the talk of the sports world: Why would Lombardi leave his spectacularly successful franchise in Green Bay and move to what was then the worst franchise in the NFL? What caught my attention was a line in the middle of the article— a pullout quote from the coach set in bold type: "I have discovered in my life that it is more challenging to build than to maintain."

I finished my coffee, drove the hour back to Haddon Heights, and told Donna that we were moving to Fort Wayne. God had vanquished my fear of failure—for the moment.

The fear returned as we spent the next few weeks

preparing our transition to Indiana. I believed God had spoken to me that day at the Jersey Shore, but I was still nervous and afraid—until we arrived. When we walked into the little house where we would live, we saw a sign taped on a kitchen cabinet door:

GOD'S COMMANDMENTS ARE GOD'S ENABLEMENTS.

To this day, I don't know who put the sign there, but I believe God moved them to do it. It suddenly dawned on me: God wouldn't tell me to do something that He wouldn't enable me to accomplish! Why should I be afraid if God had committed Himself to my success? What God did for Moses, Gideon, Jeremiah, Joshua, and others, He would do for me. And He did. For twelve years, God patiently helped me learn to be a pastor and caused the church to grow. When we left Fort Wayne, God had proved to Donna and me that the only way we learn to trust Him is to step out of our comfort zones into the "fear zone" and say yes to Him.

If you are in a similar place today, may I encourage you to replace your fear of the unknown with hope in God and His Word? If there is something God wants you to do, let your actions put your fear to flight.

CHAPTER 3

HOPE DURING A FINANCIAL COLLAPSE

Oh, fear the LORD, you His saints!
There is no want to those who fear Him.

PSALM 34:9

Ethelda Lopez was ready to let go and enjoy the golden days of her time on earth. She'd been a hard worker her whole adult life, and she had planned well for retirement. Now, when that pension check arrived each month, she felt a nice sense of security.

Then one month, the check didn't come.

It had to be a mistake. After Ethelda made a few phone calls, her discomfort increased. A Sacramento accounting firm had managed her investments, but the company was no longer to be found. Every time she phoned she got a repeated recording: "This number is no longer in service."

Ethelda had worked for AT&T for three decades. Her

benefits should have been rock solid. She'd paid into her investment plan all those years, and now she was cut off and cast adrift like a boat from its moorings. Her ultimate worst-case scenario was looming: she couldn't make the mortgage payment.

Ethelda fired off more phone calls—to mortgage companies, to her political representatives, to bank managers—to anyone at all who might be able to shed light on this craziness. But it was all to no avail. Her money was all gone—lost, embezzled, stolen. What difference did it make how it had happened? She was suddenly, unexpectedly destitute. Every night she cried herself to sleep.

Her worst fears were realized the day she stood on the lawn of the county courthouse and watched as her dream home was auctioned off to strangers. Someone wanted to know why she was crying; did she need some kind of assistance? Oh, yes. But when she tried to explain that it was her home on the auction block, nothing but unintelligible whimpers came out.

Our homes are our sanctuaries, the places where we retreat, relax, and regroup. If even this space is up for grabs, what certainties are left in the world? The idea of losing a home hits us—well, as they say—right where we live.

Loss is an inevitable part of life. Nothing that's visible is lasting, and one of the first harsh realities we face is the moment we first learn that truth. We lose a friend or we lose a job or we lose our fortune, yet life goes on.

In a very real sense, we're all nomads—pilgrims bound

for an eternal world who are just passing through this physical one. This world is not our home, and when we leave it, any possessions that outlast us will be owned by someone else. The impermanence of this world and all that is in it is actually good news for those of us who have faith in God. It means we'll be moving on to better things.

But other people live only for the here and now, as typified in Jesus' story of the prosperous but ignorant homeowner. This man placed his faith in his holdings, and then one night he heard the voice of God: "Fool! This night your soul will be required of you; then whose will those things be which you have provided?" (Luke 12:20).

The error is in thinking of home, property, and possessions as everything we have. In reality, they're the least important and most superficial of what we have. Material things dazzle us because of their one advantage: they're tangible. They can be seen, touched, and held. On the other hand, faith, hope, and the fruit of the Spirit can't be picked up and examined, bought or sold, photographed or filmed. When we allow the tangible but transient to block our perception of the invisible but imperishable, we've lost our perspective on true value.

Henry David Thoreau, the Enlightenment philosopher, understood that principle. In *Walden*, he observed that people in his village spent their lives accumulating objects that needed constant dusting. They doted on these things, even built their lives around them. Then when they died, men gathered up all their stuff, carted it to the town square, and auctioned it off to other people who would spend their lives dusting it.[1]

I am not denying the value of tangible things. Everything God created is good, including the material world (Genesis 1:31). My wife and I have a houseful of possessions, which we value at varying levels. Family pictures and heirlooms, for example, mean more to us than furnishings or automobiles. We enjoy our stuff, but we never forget that it is *stuff*. Even so, I have no desire to see it all carted to the town square. I, too, would be terribly upset to lose my home. But I know that such things can and do happen.

So the question arises: When we've lost our homes, our possessions, our bank accounts, and our investments, and the very concept of financial security has been swept away—where do we turn? Does God have anything to say that will give us comfort?

Questions don't come any more rhetorical than that, do they? *Of course* the Bible has words of comfort. The book of Psalms, our go-to book for comfort, provides a one-stop destination for all the significant emotional issues of life.

One of my favorites, Psalm 37, speaks to our hearts when the fear of calamity is stalking us. David wrote this psalm when he was an older man reflecting on the great questions of his life. Here he divides humanity into two general groups: the righteous and the wicked. Like many of us who have seen good people lose their possessions in economic recessions, David, too, has often seen bad things happen to good people and good things happen to bad people. He wants to know why. Isn't God at work, rewarding good people and striking down the bad? David thinks, considers all the evidence, and draws this conclusion:

> I have been young, and now am old;
> Yet I have not seen the righteous forsaken,
> Nor his descendants begging bread.
>
> PSALM 37:25

As David wrote this, he was well aware that wicked people were doing record business and oppressing good, God-fearing people. Earlier in the psalm he addresses this abuse, using the word *wicked* thirteen times. Here is a typical example:

> The wicked have drawn the sword
> And have bent their bow,
> To cast down the poor and needy,
> To slay those who are of upright conduct.
>
> PSALM 37:14

The term *wicked* refers to the negative moral conditions of guilt, ungodliness, and evil. It's one of those words we've more or less retired. We allow its use only for witches in fairy tales, even though we know that real wickedness abounds all around us.

How should we respond when righteous people lose their

possessions to those who are prospering through evil means? We need answers, and the Bible tells us that ultimately it's an issue of trust. Do we trust God to sort out these glaring injustices? Do we place our hope in Him more than our own finances and possessions?

Let's explore Psalm 37 and discover seven solid principles that will increase our reliance on God and anchor us in these days of instability.

Decide to Trust in the Lord

> Trust in the LORD.
>
> PSALM 37:3

One of the themes of this psalm is the principle of trusting. David uses the word *trust* three times—in verse 3, cited above, and in the two following references:

> Commit your way to the LORD,
> Trust also in Him,
> And He shall bring it to pass.
>
> PSALM 37:5

> The LORD shall help them and deliver them;
> He shall deliver them from the wicked,
> And save them,
> Because they trust in Him.
>
> PSALM 37:40

We find true stability in this unstable world only when we trust in God. To trust is to be confident—to possess a strong sense of security. When we trust, we place confidence in someone or something. Trust is not an emotion that just springs up in our hearts as does anger, jealousy, or sadness. It is always a choice based on reason. We use evidence and discernment to conclude that this man or that bank or this investment is "trustworthy." Yes, God gives us the faith to act, but He first gives us a choice to make.

To illustrate the process, let's take a look at the stock market, which is based on high-level choices of trust. If you don't trust in a company, you don't buy its stock. The stock price represents an index of the overall trust people have in a company. Wise people investigate to determine if there are grounds for trust, then they depend on God to guide their decisions. Having placed their trust in God, they need not live in fear of loss. Even if material loss occurs, God promises to meet the needs of His children, and the Bible is filled with repetitions of that promise.

For example, Psalm 23 tells us that the Lord is our Shepherd, so we shall not lack. Jesus pointed to the birds and the flowers and noted that if God feeds and clothes them, won't He do the same for His very own children (Matthew 6:25-33)? And here in Psalm 37, David tells us that in his long life, he has never seen God fail to meet needs (verse 25). His experience has proved God to be worthy of our trust. He will work things out.

Paul says the same: "My God shall supply all your need

according to His riches in glory by Christ Jesus" (Philippians 4:19). Then, in 2 Corinthians 9:8, the Lord promises that He "is able to make all grace abound toward you, that you, always having all sufficiency in all things, may have an abundance for every good work."

It's easy to say we believe in these promises, but when financial anxiety looms like an approaching storm, we're forced to confront our faith level. Do we really believe God is in control? Easy living does nothing for faith; when the weather is fine, we drift into the illusion of adequacy. We think we have it all figured out and under control.

When we find ourselves with nowhere else to turn, can God help? It's another obviously rhetorical question, isn't it? He helps by offering the only stability possible in our lives.

Christian leaders attending a YMCA convention in Carlisle, Pennsylvania, in 1873 witnessed firsthand how God can provide stability when our financial world is collapsing. Presiding over the convention was John Wanamaker, the famous retailer known today as the father of modern advertising. On the second day of the conference, a telegram arrived with shocking news. The banking house of Jay Cooke & Company had failed, resulting in terrible losses for Wanamaker and others at the convention.

When reports of other failing firms flowed into the hall, it became apparent that this was a nationwide financial crash. A tidal wave of panic swept the convention, making it hard to continue.

One of the delegates, Erastus Johnson, came across a comforting Bible verse:

From the end of the earth I will cry to You,
When my heart is overwhelmed;
Lead me to the rock that is higher than I.

PSALM 61:2

Based on that verse, Johnson wrote a song that was instantly put to music at the convention and sung over and over. It became a favorite hymn of its day, and the words are still applicable today:

Oh! Sometimes the shadows are deep,
And rough seems the path to the goal,
And sorrows, sometimes how they sweep
Like tempests down over my soul.

Oh, then to the Rock let me fly
To the Rock that is higher than I.

We've lived for too long in a world in which nothing is "higher than I." We've placed ourselves above everything else, and where has it taken us? Into a world as broken as Humpty-Dumpty—and just as impossible to put back together. The one great loss we need is the loss of the illusion that we're in any way self-sufficient. We need the Rock that is higher than we are, higher than this world. We need the Rock upon which we can make our stand, even with empty pockets, even without property or claim, even without a shred of worldly hope, because at the end of our vain hope lies the beginning of the knowledge of God and His grace.

Another great hymn says, "On Christ the solid rock I stand/All other ground is sinking sand." When the sinking sand of nest eggs and 401(k) plans destroys our sand castle, nothing but trust in God provides stability.

Trust in God will not make the pain go away; it means we know He will provide what we truly need. In Christ our hope stands tall, solid, and untouchable. In Him we have a home that outshines the sun, an inheritance that can never perish, and treasures that can never be taken from us. The deed to our heavenly home is signed and sealed with the blood of Christ; the contract is ratified by the Resurrection. And no one will ever foreclose on that.

Do Things That Honor the Lord

Trust in the LORD, and do good.
PSALM 37:3

Here David tells us that we respond to God first by trusting and then by doing good—trust and obey. Trust is an act of the mind, while obedience is an act of the hands and feet. Once we've set our minds on the wisdom of God, we get busy doing the things He would have us do. It's simple but empowering: "Trust in the LORD, and do good."

Let's look first at the trust step—the "think right" step. Paul's advice to his protégé, Timothy, captures it well:

"Godliness with contentment is great gain. For we brought nothing into this world, and it is certain we can carry nothing out. And having food and clothing, with these we shall be content" (1 Timothy 6:6-8).

Godliness with contentment is the mindset for right thinking—the pinnacle of wisdom in the Christian life. Don't crave more than you need; demonstrate your trust in God by being content with what you have. It's why Paul could be stripped of all he owned and thrown into prison, yet still manifest incredible joy. The world is filled with wealthy, miserable people who have everything but contentment. Their money is an empty god that can never fill the vacuum in their souls with peace. Here Paul points those with money toward right thinking: "Command those who are rich in this present age not to be haughty, nor to trust in uncertain riches but in the living God, who gives us richly all things to enjoy. Let them do good, that they be rich in good works, ready to give, willing to share, storing up for themselves a good foundation for the time to come" (1 Timothy 6:17-19).

Paul stresses the idea of both thinking rightly (trust) and then acting rightly (obedience). Right thinking means trusting in an unshakable God instead of riches that we can't take with us. Right acting means doing good, which builds a heavenly nest egg of riches waiting just for us.

These insights echo throughout the Scriptures, and they are summed up in Paul's restatement of Job's famous observation: "We brought nothing into this world, and it is certain we can carry nothing out" (1 Timothy 6:7). Someone has observed that life is ultimately like a board game of Monopoly: you go around a few times; you collect paper money and houses; and then, sooner or later, it all goes back in the box.

What we often hear of wealth is true: you can't take it with you. But you can send it on ahead. Jesus said we can lay up treasures in heaven. That means we can live now in a way that earns a kind of interest for the next life. Whenever we serve a fellow human being, we're earning that kind of spiritual capital. Jesus said that even giving a cup of cold water to someone in need is rewarded in heaven (Matthew 10:42). He also said that when we amass "treasures in heaven," no moth can eat them away, and no robber can steal them (Matthew 6:19-20).

The great Christian leader John Wesley lived in a time of financial disruption, and he took those words of Jesus very seriously. The Industrial Revolution was causing a massive move to the cities. Farms were lost, small-town economies collapsed, and epidemics of crime and disease plagued the cities. The rich grew richer, and the poor grew in number.

Wesley saw the crowds of hurting people as Jesus would see them, and he designed ministries to care for them. His ministry became a financial success, and his annual salary grew to be the modern-day equivalent of $160,000. Wesley calculated the small sum that he really needed and gave the rest away. He saw it as investing in the things of God, which never perish. Wesley said, "If I leave behind me ten pounds, . . . you and all mankind [can] bear witness against me, that I have lived and died a thief and a robber."[2]

By no means was John Wesley against the idea of wealth; his problem was with "storing up treasures on earth" when wealth could be such a marvelous tool for ministry. He once preached a sermon in which he proposed the best attitude we can have toward wealth: "Gain all you can, save all you can, give all you can."[3]

When we do things that honor the Lord, we invest in eternity.

Dwell on the Faithfulness of the Lord

Feed on His faithfulness.

PSALM 37:3

Your mercy, O LORD, is in the heavens;
Your faithfulness reaches to the clouds.

PSALM 36:5

These verses draw our attention to the faithfulness of the Lord. But let's take a peek at the final verse of Psalm 37 to learn the outcome of God's faithfulness:

The LORD shall help them and deliver them;
He shall deliver them from the wicked,
And save them,
Because they trust in Him.

PSALM 37:40

To trust in Him is to respond in faith to His faithfulness. David knew from experience that God rewards faith with blessings. As a young man, David had been anointed as the next king of Israel. Then he spent years living in forests and caves as the reigning king hunted him down. He had to do more than merely assent to the idea of God's faithfulness—he had to stake his life on it. Life was hard during those long, perilous years. But in time, Saul died, David became king, and he could attest to the fact that God keeps His promises.

Timothy George, the dean of Beeson Divinity School, recalls a story from one of his professors, Dr. Gardner Taylor, who had once preached in Louisiana. He had been assigned to a poor, rural church with a sanctuary lit by a single lightbulb hanging from the ceiling. One evening he was preaching the Gospel with gusto when suddenly the power went out. Dr. Taylor had no idea what the protocol might be, so he stumbled around in the dark until an elderly deacon cried out, "Preach on, brother! We can still see Jesus in the dark!"

Sometimes, George concludes, we see Him *best* in the dark. "And the good news of the gospel is that whether or not we can see him in the dark, he can see us in the dark."[4]

Delight Yourself in the Lord

> Delight yourself also in the LORD,
> And He shall give you the desires of your heart.
>
> PSALM 37:4

Even when our circumstances hold nothing delightful for us, we find delight in the Lord. We could be facing loss and oppression, but these things don't define us. Because we put our hope in God, we find an inner joy in Him.

What gives you delight? The word refers to extreme satisfaction or gratification. I find delight in a good football game or in Frank Sinatra singing a terrific old song. I find deeper delight in having my family all around and hearing about what's new in the world of my grandchildren. One of my deepest delights is time alone with my wife, my soul mate of all these years. No one on earth knows me as she does, and we create our own little world when we're together.

But my deepest delight is found in the Lord. I can go to Him no matter what is happening in my world, and the amazing truth is that He finds delight in me. I can't even begin to imagine why, but He does. My children and grandchildren realize that there's never a time when I'm not overjoyed to see them. God has this kind of delight in His children, and we should delight in Him—not because we "ought to" but because there is no deeper joy in life.

David squeezed every drop out of life the way some do an orange. He had many delights, many gifts. He could sing, he could dance, he could write poetry, he could devise battle plans, and he had an aching desire to design a temple for God. He was a passionate man who found the best in life, and he wanted us to know that one's greatest delight is found in the knowledge of God. And as usual, there's a breathtaking promise attached to that delight. The promise is that if we delight ourselves in the Lord, He will give us the desires of our hearts. Can anything so wonderful be true? Absolutely! But it's important to understand this promise. It isn't a short-cut to prosperity, as some ill-informed preachers claim. We don't delight in the Lord *so that* He will give us what we want. That approach confuses faith with greed.

No, when we find true and genuine pleasure in God, with no thought of gain other than gaining intimacy with Him, we find our own desires coming into conformance with His desires. We begin to live in His will, and we pray accordingly. We find the joy of the Lord by following the Lord of joy into His joy. The following promises capture this idea:

> He said to them, "Go your way, eat the fat, drink the sweet, and send portions to those for whom nothing is prepared; for this day is holy to our Lord. Do not sorrow, for the joy of the LORD is your strength."
>
> NEHEMIAH 8:10

> You will show me the path of life;
> In Your presence is fullness of joy;
> At Your right hand are pleasures forevermore.
>
> PSALM 16:11

When things go wrong and loss overtakes us, misery often follows. And the more we struggle against the pit of discouragement, the deeper it becomes. But if we've placed our hope in God no matter what, His joy becomes our strength.

We delight in Him and find new energy, new insights, and new resources to keep on going.

How can we delight in God or anything else when our world is crashing down on us? We can begin by turning to Psalm 119, which uses the word *delight* six times and shows us the first step in finding it.

> *I will delight myself in Your statutes;*
> *I will not forget Your word.*
> PSALM 119:16

> *Make me walk in the path of Your commandments,*
> *For I delight in it.*
> PSALM 119:35

> *The proud have forged a lie against me,*
> *But I will keep Your precepts with my whole heart.*
> *Their heart is as fat as grease,*
> *But I delight in Your law.*
> PSALM 119:69-70

> *Let Your tender mercies come to me, that I may live;*
> *For Your law is my delight.*
> PSALM 119:77

> *Unless Your law had been my delight,*
> *I would then have perished in my affliction.*
> PSALM 119:92

I long for Your salvation, O LORD,
And Your law is my delight.

PSALM 119:174

Did you pick up on the common theme these six verses express? The first step in delighting in God is to delight in His Word. Immersing ourselves in the Word of God reveals a God we can delight in. The psalmist takes such a delight in God's Word that he uses every possible term to express the range of its meaning: statutes, commandments, precepts, law. In the same way, other writers of Scripture delight in God by using His various names. Isn't that just what people do when they're in love? They come up with pet names for their beloved, and each name has a special meaning that conveys a particular facet of the delight they find.

Delighting in God's Word leads us to delight in God, and delight in God drives away fear.

Dedicate Your Life to the Lord

Commit your way to the LORD,
Trust also in Him,
And He shall bring it to pass.

PSALM 37:5

Having found our deepest delight in God, we realize that we must give *all* of our lives to Him. This isn't a temporary commitment, a halfway intention, or the feeling of a moment.

It's a choice and a contract of the heart. As in marriage, we commit ourselves to that partnership for the rest of our lives.

How does committing to the Lord help us in times of material loss? In committing to Him, we cast all our burdens upon Him. He becomes our life—the place where we bring our problems, our joys, our marriages, our families, our careers. Life and happiness are no longer dependent on financial success or material possessions. It's now all about Him.

The verse above ends with the phrase "And He shall bring it to pass." When we put our hope in Him, depend on Him, and respond to Him in faith, He will make our greatest dreams come true by elevating them from the material to the eternal.

God is also the answer when our losses leave us unable to help ourselves:

> *The helpless commits himself to You;*
> *You are the helper of the fatherless.*
> PSALM 10:14

When we dedicate ourselves to God, *helpless* becomes a word without meaning. When we've lost our jobs, our houses, or our savings, and debt or bankruptcy stares us in the face, it's as if we're crushed under the weight of an enormous sack filled with every problem facing us. It's a burden too heavy to bear. We can't take another step. We can't lift it—but God can. He gently says, "May I take that upon

Myself? My shoulders are stronger." As we say yes, life brightens and becomes joyful.

> Cast your burden on the LORD,
> And He shall sustain you;
> He shall never permit the righteous to be moved.
> PSALM 55:22

> [Cast] all your care upon Him, for He cares for you.
> 1 PETER 5:7

Why keep struggling with your losses on your own? Why not give the burden to Him? Nothing could be more liberating.

William Carey, the "father of modern missions," established a large print shop in Serampore, India, where he worked for years translating the Bible into many Indian languages.

On March 11, 1812, Carey had to travel to another town. His associate, William Ward, was working late when suddenly he smelled smoke. He leaped up to discover black clouds belching from the printing room. He screamed for help, and workers carried water from the nearby river until 2 a.m. But it was to no avail; nearly everything was destroyed.

The next day, missionary Joshua Marshman entered a Calcutta classroom where Carey was teaching. He placed a gentle hand on his friend's shoulder and said, "I can think of no easy way to break the news. The print shop burned to the ground last night."

Gone was Carey's massive translation work of nearly twenty years: a dictionary, two grammar books, and whole versions of the Bible. Gone were sets of type for fourteen Eastern languages, twelve hundred reams of paper, fifty-five thousand printed sheets, and thirty pages of his Bengal dictionary. Gone was his complete library. "The work of years— gone in a moment," he whispered.

In that moment he understood the pain of loss. "The loss is heavy," he wrote, "but as traveling a road the second time is usually done with greater ease and certainty than the first time, so I trust the work will lose nothing of real value. We are not discouraged; indeed the work is already begun again in every language. We are cast down but not in despair."

William Carey had dedicated his life to God, and he trusted Him to bring blessings in the ashes of his dreams. "There are grave difficulties on every hand," he once wrote, "and more are looming ahead. Therefore we must go forward." As Carey moved forward, so did God. News of the fire caused all England to start talking about William Carey. Money for support flowed in. Volunteers enlisted to help. The print shop was rebuilt and enlarged.

By 1832, complete Bibles, New Testaments, or separate books of Scripture had issued from the press in forty-four languages and dialects.[5]

Because Carey had dedicated his life to God, he understood what it meant to cast all his burdens on the Lord, even when all seemed lost.

Download Your Worry to the Lord

Do not fret because of him who prospers in his way,
Because of the man who brings wicked schemes to pass.
PSALM 37:7

Times of economic chaos produce anxiety, and for believers, these times can become a real challenge to faith.

Remember, there are two strategies for facing the future: with fear or with faith. If you've decided to follow Christ, that means walking by faith (2 Corinthians 5:7). That does not mean Satan will forget about you. He will try to chip away at your faith by pointing you to the fear of the moment. At this time in our nation, that fear focuses heavily on finances. But fear about money—or about anything, for that matter—is never part of God's plan for us. As Paul writes, "God has not given us a spirit of fear, but of power and of love and of a sound mind" (2 Timothy 1:7). Embed this verse in your mind, and bring it to the forefront whenever you feel that first pang of fear.

Many other Bible promises will strengthen your faith and help you overcome the fear of the moment:

- Romans 8:35-39 assures us that nothing is able to separate us from the love of God.
- First John 4:18 reminds us that God's perfect love casts out our fear.
- Philippians 4:6-7 invites us to lay our anxieties before God by faith with thanksgiving, allowing the peace of God to guard our hearts and minds in Christ Jesus.

We need to understand that faith in God does not immunize us from financial failure. As long as we live in this fallen world, there will be no such thing as complete financial security. There is no ultimate security in anything but the grace of God. To be human means that loss, including heartbreaking loss, is always possible. As tough as times are, they can and may become much worse. But faith in God assures us that He holds our lives in His powerful, loving hands, which means no collapses, no losses, and no fears can truly harm us. As the Lord of this universe, He is, indeed, too big to fail.

Because God loves and cares for us, David urges us not to worry, or as he puts it, "Do not fret." This phrase *do not fret* essentially means "relax; don't react." It occurs only four times in the entire Bible—three times in Psalm 37 and once in Proverbs.

- Psalm 37:1: "Do not fret because of evildoers."
- Psalm 37:7: "Do not fret because of him who prospers in his way."
- Psalm 37:8: "Do not fret—it only causes harm."
- Proverbs 24:19: "Do not fret because of evildoers, nor be envious of the wicked."

The English word *fret* comes from the Old English *fretan*, meaning "to devour, to eat, to gnaw into something." The Hebrew word David used is *charah*, which has at its root the idea of "growing warm" and "blazing up."

Here we have a mix of two metaphors illustrating the same idea—a word picture of gnawing and a word picture of fire. In the first metaphor, fretting is seen as a rat inside your soul, gnawing away at your joy and peace. (I didn't say it was a pretty picture. But it's a true one.)

The fire metaphor pictures Satan as the arsonist of hellfire, setting blazes of distress inside your heart. Both pictures illustrate the destructiveness of fretting. In Psalm 37 David tells us not to put up with fretting: kill the rats and douse the fires, because fretting will kill you from the inside out.

Someone has observed that the prosperous people of the previous generation known as the "jet set" have now become the "fret set." Once they were flying high, and now they're flying off the handle.

One of the most frustrating things about massive losses is that we look around and see evil people prospering—sometimes even because of their evil. It violates our sense of justice. But in Psalm 37 David assures us that justice will be done. God is not yet finished with these people. Five times in this psalm, David gives us reason not to envy the prosperous wicked:

> They shall soon be cut down like the grass,
> And wither as the green herb.
>
> PSALM 37:2

> For yet a little while and the wicked shall be no more;
> Indeed, you will look carefully for his place,
> But it shall be no more.
>
> PSALM 37:10

> The wicked shall perish;
> And the enemies of the LORD,
> Like the splendor of the meadows, shall vanish.
> Into smoke they shall vanish away.
>
> PSALM 37:20

> When the wicked are cut off, you shall see it.
>
> PSALM 37:34

> I have seen the wicked in great power,
> And spreading himself like a native green tree.
> Yet he passed away, and behold, he was no more;
> Indeed I sought him, but he could not be found.
>
> PSALM 37:35-36

As a creative exercise, pastor and author Leonard Griffith transplanted Rip Van Winkle, the beloved Washington Irving character, into 1930s Germany. You remember the story: Rip falls asleep for twenty years, then walks through town to find that everything has changed and no one remembers him.

In Griffith's version, Van Winkle is horrified as he watches Hitler rise to power and begin conquering Europe. He retreats into the Alps to get away from the terrifying events. There he falls asleep. When he wakes up, the 1950s are underway and the world is vastly different. The Nazis are gone—no more swastikas, no more eager Hitler youth, no more arrogant attitudes of world domination. The masterminds of the Third Reich are all dead or imprisoned or being hunted down.

Rip Van Winkle then understands the words of the psalmist: "I have seen the wicked in great power, and spreading himself like a native green tree. Yet he passed away, and behold, he was no more."[6]

Many in the 1930s wondered why God allowed the Nazis to prosper. He didn't. He dealt with them by His own timetable, and He dealt with them thoroughly.

There's another point to be considered here. What if the wrong people do come out on top in this life? Would we really want to trade our kind of security for theirs? Spurgeon wrote, "What if wicked devices succeed and your own plans are defeated! There is more of the love of God in your defeats than in the successes of the wicked."[7]

Discipline Yourself to Wait on the Lord

Rest in the LORD, and wait patiently for Him.

PSALM 37:7

Waiting doesn't come easily for us. In this age of instant gratification, we're conditioned not to wait for anything. If the fast-food line is too long, we rush to the restaurant across the street. If the TV show doesn't quickly become interesting, we surf impatiently through hundreds of channels. If the car ahead doesn't move the instant the traffic light changes, we hit the horn.

When we face loss, we know we must trust God's timetable for dealing with it. But what we'd like better is for Him to accede to ours. The fact that we cannot see into the future can convince us that the future is up for grabs. But rest assured, God is completely in control. Though His timing may seem slow to us, from the viewpoint of eternity, it is perfect. God is never early and never late.

When we truly believe this, we acquire the mind of Christ, which enables us to wait on Him with patience and trust. Waiting means . . .

- Not lagging behind His leading and direction
- Not walking ahead of His leading and direction
- Not ignoring His leading and direction
- Not fretting about what He is doing or planning for you

The word *wait* is found two additional times in this psalm:

Evildoers shall be cut off;
But those who wait on the LORD,
They shall inherit the earth.
PSALM 37:9

Wait on the LORD,
And keep His way,
And He shall exalt you to inherit the land.
PSALM 37:34

Waiting is difficult in the face of loss, but it's a discipline with a huge payoff. Those who wait on the Lord will "inherit the earth" because those pushers and shovers in life's express line have all burned out, victims of their own impatience. Patient people are happier and healthier, and God will exalt them.

One writer explained that there are two kinds of faith: one based on *if* and the other on *though*. The first says, "*If* everything goes the way I want, then I'll agree that God is good." The other says, "*Though* evil may prosper, *though* I may sweat in Gethsemane, *though* my road leads to Calvary—even so, I trust in God." The first wants instant results; the second has learned the wisdom of waiting, as Job did when he cried out, "Though He slay me, yet will I trust Him" (Job 13:15).[8]

Almost two hundred years ago, our nation went through

economic upheaval: the Panic of 1837. Anna and Susan Warner and their father, Henry Warner, lived in a mansion filled with art treasures, high-class furnishings, and an army of servants. Then came the deluge.

The market crashed and took Henry Warner's investments down with it. The family lost everything and, deeply in debt, moved to a decrepit old house up the river from New York City. Henry's financial collapse devastated him emotionally, and he was never the same. The daughters, accustomed to expensive parties and the social whirl, now realized they had to pitch in to work down the family's staggering debt.

All they could think to do was write. Though they struggled to find a publisher, eventually Putnam accepted Susan Warner's novel *The Wide, Wide World*. Success followed. The sisters wrote more than one hundred books, all built on the foundation of the Gospel that warmed their lives. One of the books, *Say and Seal*, contained a little poem Anna had woven into the story. It began with the words "Jesus loves me, this I know." Songwriter William Bradbury added music, and now "Jesus Loves Me" is loved throughout the world. Untold millions of children have first encountered Christ through its simple yet powerful words. In 1943, when John F. Kennedy's PT-109 was sunk in the Solomon Islands, local islanders and American marines sang the song as they rescued the survivors. You may have sung it as a child. I did.

If you had been part of this disconsolate family, standing in the ashes of financial failure and watching as your lifetime possessions were hauled away, you might have thought that life was unfair. But if you knew the ways of God, you might have known even then that He had special things in mind. From the cold rubble and debris of today's misfortune, God raises the bricks and beams of tomorrow's miracle.

Yes, we know that "all things work together for good to those who love God" (Romans 8:28), but this long-term promise does not provide a quick fix for the heartbreak of loss. There's no bypass to avoid it. Yet the promise remains true, and it gives us something to cling to and focus on through the blur of our tears.

The devil may win today, but the God who owns tomorrow "works out everything in conformity with the purpose of his will, in order that we, who were the first to put our hope in Christ, might be for the praise of his glory" (Ephesians 1:11-12, NIV).

Philip Yancey points out that two of the primary days we've named on the church calendar are Good Friday and Easter Sunday. One held the worst event imaginable, and the other the greatest. Yet we live most of life on the day between—Saturday—a day we've given no special name. Like the disciples, we sit in the wake of life's heartbreak with no clue that what the morning will bring is brighter than our most brilliant dreams.

Life is about deciding how to live in that interim between cross and crown. Just how much do we trust God? Do we really believe He can take a world that includes genocide in Bosnia and Rwanda, inner-city ghettos, capacity prisons, and wipe out losses, then fashion something beautiful out of it? We know what Friday feels like. Is there going to be a Sunday?

Yancey observes that the day of Christ's beatings, crucifixion, and death is called *Good* Friday. It only earns that adjective in light of Sunday's developments. The empty tomb refashions the shame of the Cross into a victory. Easter, says Yancey, offers a clue into the greater workings of God. Our souls rise above the loss of Friday, knowing that blessing will come on Sunday. In the meantime, Saturday becomes a day of waiting.[9]

Waiting is not always a bad thing; it can bring its own joy—the thrill of anticipation. Do you remember waiting for Christmas as a child? Waiting for your wedding day? Waiting for something good makes the heart sing. It fills us with hope. It changes us internally so that the ups and downs of this fickle, undependable life can exert no real power over us. The world may take away our homes and every cent we have. We may cry out, but our hope is intact because our losses are only a reminder of the grand gift that, once received, can never be lost. And it's worth waiting for.

CHAPTER 4

HOPE AMID
SERIOUS ILLNESS

I, the LORD your God, will hold your right hand,
saying to you, "Fear not, I will help you."

ISAIAH 41:13

As I write this chapter, I have just completed my semi-annual CT scan. For nearly twenty years, I've been making this round-trip journey to the Scripps Clinic in La Jolla, California. It all began in 1994 when I was diagnosed with non-Hodgkin's lymphoma at the Mayo Clinic in Rochester, Minnesota. I arranged to receive chemotherapy at Scripps, nearer to my home. With each passing year, the staff there has risen higher on my list of heroes.

It was on my first day at Scripps that I met Dr. Alan Saven, the oncologist. After two decades, he still examines me twice yearly. He and Dr. Charles Mason, who presided over my stem cell transplant, saved my life.

Make no mistake, to *God* be the glory—He and only He holds my life in His hands. But I also know that He raises up caring and gifted people to apply their skills as God's agents in delivering His gift of health. I'm so grateful for these talented specialists, and I let them know it in every way I can.

I won't recount all the details of my bout with cancer. You can find them in my book *When Your World Falls Apart.* But here in this book about hope in the face of fear, I can't help but revisit those memories. People know I'm a pastor, and they know my thoughts on spiritual issues. Therefore they want to know whether I was afraid as I struggled with cancer. I'm more than happy to answer that question, but I must warn you that it may be difficult for you to truly understand what I'm saying. Cancer is one of those subjects that can't be comprehended secondhand. It's larger than life; it carries such powerful implications that it changes a person forever. Whenever I open the door at Scripps, the feelings come flooding back, even though I've had consistently good reports for two decades. The good news never quite washes out the memory and emotions of those uncertain times. So was I afraid? Is it fear that comes creeping back even now? Here's what I wrote in that previous book:

> Absolutely! I was *desperately* afraid. There's no
> disputing that. Was I afraid to die? No. I'm not
> afraid to leave this life, although I'm not eager to do
> so either. A good bit of my fear focused on losing
> precious years with the people I love. Some of it

was simply about pain. Some of it was about the unknown. How would you respond to the news that you were suffering from a possibly fatal disease? Imagine the thoughts and feelings that might flood your heart at such a time, and you'll know the same things I experienced.[1]

Missionary Isobel Kuhn wrote a book entitled *In the Arena*, in which she explains a wonderful truth: a life filled with problems and setbacks can become a life filled with unique tools for sharing the Gospel. Every issue she faced brought one more opportunity to glorify God through the wisdom she learned.

In her final chapter, Isobel told of how she coped with breast cancer. Health became her great concern, and knowing how cancer could spread, her natural impulse was to panic—to anticipate the worst. If she coughed, it must be lung cancer. A toothache meant mouth cancer. Every minor ache or twinge was a harbinger of dire health consequences. She learned that disease is the host of fear.[2]

Eventually, however, Isobel learned that Christ overcomes every fear. That message can change the world, and it can change your life.

The Prevalence of Disease

It's hard for us to imagine anyone living in perfect health, but Adam and Eve did. Their bodies were absolutely flawless.

The very concept of disease would have been foreign to them. Their sin, of course, shattered that reality. It cost them God's gift of perfection and corrupted the whole created order. As Paul tells us, God's creation, now afflicted with disease and corruption, groans in agony (Romans 8:20-22). Because of Adam and Eve's rebellion, disease is now a prevalent factor of our existence. Each of us will spend a certain portion of our lives sick, wounded, or dying.

We view sickness with revulsion and dread, and somewhere in our spirits we sense that things weren't meant to be this way. God has placed eternity in our hearts, and thus threats to life come as odious intrusions. We long for the day when the curse of sin will be lifted—"eagerly waiting for the adoption, the redemption of our body" (Romans 8:23). Until then, we must cope with the inevitability of bodily corruption.

As we lose the naive sense of invulnerability of youth, we fret over aches and pains and what they may foretell. We feel anxious over the doctor's call with a test result or the look on his face as he walks into the room. We panic over a strange feeling in the chest or a lump where none should be. These are basic, primal fears. Death does its work in increments: the erosion of teeth, the growing inflexibility of limbs, the dulling of the senses. There are only so many ways to do maintenance work on the human body. We jog, we work out, we eat right, and then, as comedian Redd Foxx put it, someday we lie down in a hospital, "dying of nothing."

The diversity of the human body allows many points of

entry for the grim reaper. According to the Federal Centers for Disease Control, the leading causes of death by disease in the United States are (in descending order) heart disease, cancer, respiratory diseases, stroke, Alzheimer's disease, diabetes, kidney disease, and pneumonia.[3]

Not only do diseases take a physical and an emotional toll, they take a financial one as well. The United States is the most expensive nation when it comes to treating illness.[4] In just one year, the total cost for health care was more than $3.6 trillion.[5] Because of these astronomical costs, a major medical incident can wipe out a family living on the financial edge. When our bodily health declines, so does the health of our wallets.

Disease (*dis-ease*) literally means "not easy" or "not at ease." Our experiences confirm the accuracy of that definition. Disease disrupts the patterns of life, robbing us of control and forming barriers with other people. It sends us to expensive medical facilities where we place our fate in the hands of strangers. It builds our dependence on mystifying medications. Commercials for these medicines show happy, healthy people who don't seem to have a care in the world. But at the end of the ad, the announcer lists ominous side effects in a hushed voice and with the speed of an auctioneer on steroids.

Hospitals are not fun places. They're a conglomeration of needles, tubes, monitors, pills, thermometers, call buttons, and bedpans—not to mention the total absence of modesty and privacy.

We all fear disease, yet one or more will eventually catch up with each of us. Maybe you're battling an illness right now. Maybe it's just around the next corner, or perhaps someone dear to you is fighting desperately for his or her health. Disease is prevalent and inevitable, but how we understand it makes a great difference. It's no surprise that the Bible has a great deal to say about disease and how people coped with it.

Prominent Biblical Examples of Disease

I've never preached a sermon series on "Diseased Characters from the Bible," nor has any pastor I know. But there would be a wealth of material to mine. For example:

- Paul and his "thorn in the flesh," which may have been a physical illness (2 Corinthians 12:7)
- Job sitting in his ash heap, covered with boils (Job 2:7-8)
- Lazarus, a young man with a terminal illness (John 11:1-4)
- The woman with the issue of blood (Mark 5:25-29)
- Naaman and his leprosy (2 Kings 5:1)
- King David and the "evil disease" that clung to him (Psalm 41:8)
- King Asa and his foot disease (1 Kings 15:23)
- King Jehoram and his diseased intestines (2 Chronicles 21:15)

- Christ's Galilean friends with "all kinds of sickness and all kinds of disease" (Matthew 4:23)
- Epaphroditus, who was "sick almost unto death" (Philippians 2:26-27)
- Dorcas, who fell sick, died, and was raised from death by Peter (Acts 9:36-41)

As we read of people in Scripture who suffered with various diseases, we recognize the same emotions we feel today. One compelling example is Hezekiah, a king of Judah. Let's look first at his life, and then we'll explore his approach to illness. His battle with disease is recounted three times: in 2 Kings 20, 2 Chronicles 32, and Isaiah 38.

Hezekiah was one of Judah's greatest kings. "He trusted in the LORD God of Israel, so that after him was none like him among all the kings of Judah, nor who were before him" (2 Kings 18:5).

Hezekiah ascended the throne at the age of twenty-five and inspired a period of religious revival in which he was encouraged by Isaiah, perhaps the noblest and the most eloquent of the Hebrew prophets. Hezekiah opened the long-closed doors of the Temple in Jerusalem and began its renovation, issuing this charge to the priests and Levites: "Hear me, Levites! Now sanctify yourselves, sanctify the house of the LORD God of your fathers, and carry out the rubbish from the holy place" (2 Chronicles 29:5).

The final verses of this great chapter describe the lavish Temple consecration services and the joy of the king and his people, who felt that God was doing a great thing among them. (Reading this account makes us long for a similar revival today.) In chapter 30, we learn that God's hand was on this nation, bringing its people together in unity and obedience under God. We find a glowing summary of Hezekiah's reign in 2 Chronicles 31:20-21:

> Hezekiah did . . . what was good and right and true before the LORD his God. And in every work that he began in the service of the house of God, in the law and in the commandment, to seek his God, he did it with all his heart. So he prospered.

It was a golden age of faith and prosperity in Judah, and all things went well for ten to fifteen years. Then, when Hezekiah turned thirty-nine, he became ill. The prophet Isaiah came to him and said, "Thus says the LORD: 'Set your house in order, for you shall die and not live'" (Isaiah 38:1).

Painful Emotions of Disease

How would you react if you learned that your death was imminent? If a godly man like Hezekiah "wept bitterly" (Isaiah 38:3), then we can understand it's no sin to express grief when we're hit with terrible medical news. Hezekiah was not just a godly king; he was a godly *human* king. And humans naturally grieve in the face of bad news. As we follow the progress of Hezekiah's illness, we'll gather helpful insights into the art of managing poor health.

The Prayer

> Hezekiah turned his face toward the wall, and prayed to the LORD, and said, "Remember now, O LORD, I pray, how I have walked before You in truth and with a loyal heart, and have done what is good in Your sight." And Hezekiah wept bitterly.
>
> ISAIAH 38:2-3

Hezekiah, horrified and in earnest grief, soaked his sickbed with sweat and tears. Later he wrote a memoir of his illness, which we find in Isaiah 38:10-15. The first few verses of that passage offer a vivid and wrenching picture of Hezekiah's troubled heart. Here, in Eugene Peterson's memorable paraphrase, are the reflections of this king upon the news of his impending death:

> In the very prime of life
> > I have to leave.
> Whatever time I have left
> > is spent in death's waiting room.
> No more glimpses of GOD
> > in the land of the living,
> No more meetings with my neighbors,
> > no more rubbing shoulders with friends.

This body I inhabit is taken down
    and packed away like a camper's tent.
Like a weaver, I've rolled up the carpet of my life
    as God cuts me free of the loom
And at day's end sweeps up the scraps and pieces.
    I cry for help until morning.
Like a lion, God pummels and pounds me,
    relentlessly finishing me off.
I squawk like a doomed hen,
    moan like a dove.
My eyes ache from looking up for help:
    "Master, I'm in trouble! Get me out of this!"
But what's the use? God Himself gave me the word.
    He's done it to me.
I can't sleep—
    I'm that upset, that troubled.

ISAIAH 38:10-15, *THE MESSAGE*

In my own memoir of illness, I shared that it took me three days simply to be capable of telling my wife the doctor's news. On the day after my diagnosis, she was scheduled to leave town to visit her mother, and I decided not to burden her. I knew she'd immediately cancel her trip, and for what? There was no point in disturbing her until further tests were done.

So I kept my silence. I drove her to the airport the next day, watched her plane vanish into the clouds, and suddenly felt the pangs of loneliness; it was time to confront the dark jungle of my thoughts. I longed for her comfort, but it would only be a three-day wait. We met in another city where I was scheduled to speak, and that's where I quietly told her what the doctors had said.

We wept, but not bitterly. Even at such a low moment, we knew we had our faith and we had each other. We held each other for hours as the gray dusk of a new morning gathered outside.

During my previous three days of solitary meditation, I walked in Hezekiah's sandals. *Master, I'm in trouble—get me out of this!* I prayed, just as Jesus prayed for the cup to be taken from Him. But just as He set His own desires within the will of the Father (Luke 22:42), I knew what all serious Christians know: my prayers would cycle through a process that would end at the same destination: *Your will, not mine, O Lord.*

I'm not comparing my plight to that of the Son of God, of course. I just followed His example to the resolution I knew was inevitable. His will, I knew, is infinitely wiser than my feeble comprehension. The cycle of every anguished prayer must move from our frantic human desires to loving, trusting obedience.

Tears and prayer are understandable responses to disease, whether we're the one afflicted or we're grieving for a loved one. Though we can't predict how the Lord will answer, we know the tears and prayers of His suffering people always move Him (Psalm 56:8).

The Promise

> The word of the LORD came to Isaiah, saying, "Go and tell Hezekiah, 'Thus says the LORD, the God of David your father: "I have heard your prayer, I have seen your tears; surely I will add to your days fifteen years."'"
>
> ISAIAH 38:4-5

Here Hezekiah received the joyful news he was longing to hear: God would heal him. Why did God do this? Why did he heal the king and give him fifteen more years of life? In part, it was because He saw Hezekiah's tears and was moved by compassion.

Recall the basis of Hezekiah's prayer for healing: "Remember now, O LORD, I pray, how I have walked before You in truth and with a loyal heart, and have done what is good in Your sight" (Isaiah 38:3). Hezekiah laid out his case before God: "I've been faithful to You. I've cleansed the land of idols and restored the Temple worship. So in return, please be gracious and heal me."

We must remember, however, that no matter how great a king Hezekiah was, God had no obligation to heal him. We cannot earn His favor with our works. God's healing is about His faithfulness, not ours. Healing comes the same way salvation does—by grace: "By [the Messiah's] stripes we are healed" (Isaiah 53:5). Healing is part of the very nature of God, and in His grace, He offers it to those who fear Him: "To you who fear My name the Sun of Righteousness shall arise with healing in His wings" (Malachi 4:2).

We find another reason for Hezekiah's healing in Isaiah 38:5: God said to the king: "Thus says the LORD, the God of David your father." God had made a covenant with David that the throne of Judah would always go to one of David's descendants. The reference to David in this passage is God's reminder that He is faithful to His promises. That faithfulness was demonstrated when, three years after Hezekiah's healing, his son Manasseh, who would be the next king, was born (2 Chronicles 33:1).

After Hezekiah was healed, God reminded him again of His faithfulness to His promise to David. He said He would defend Jerusalem against the invading Assyrians "for My own sake and for My servant David's sake" (2 Kings 19:34).

God's dealings with Hezekiah and his nation were part of a much bigger story than Hezekiah could see. It was also about the glory of God—as it always is—and about a promise made long ago to David. God is always good, gracious, and compassionate, and therefore He is a worthy place to put our hope.

Why does God heal us? Essentially for the same reasons He healed Hezekiah: first, because of His grace and compassion, and second, for the sake of Jesus Christ—a son of David. Like Hezekiah's story, ours also is part of a much greater one that we cannot yet see.

The Prescription

Isaiah had said, "Let them take a lump of figs, and apply it as a poultice on the boil, and he shall recover."

ISAIAH 38:21

Hezekiah's fatal disease stemmed from a boil somewhere on his body. We can probably assume it had become infected and was leaching poison into his system. God gave Isaiah directions for healing, which were to be passed on to the court physicians attending the king.

The prescription was a poultice (or paste) made of crushed figs to be applied to the boil. It's not likely that today's physicians would think of using pharmaceutical figs, which might be seen as alternative or herbal medicine. It's more likely they would lance and drain the boil, then administer an antibiotic.

You might wonder why God bothered to use the court physicians at all. Why not heal Hezekiah through a simple miracle? But God has a habit of using people, their gifts, and their resources to carry out His plans. In fact, we were created to be God's deputies, doing His work on earth (Genesis 1:28). As C. S. Lewis said, God "seems to do nothing of Himself which He can possibly delegate to His creatures."[6] Clearly, God used doctors and prescriptions in Hezekiah's time just as He does now.

In 1994, doctors treated my lymphoma with chemotherapy. When the lymphoma returned in 1998, I received a stem cell transplant. That's the scientific part of the story. But behind the scenes, a great many people were praying for my recovery. That's the faith part of the story.

This raises a question. How much of my healing should be credited to medicine, and how much to prayer? We can't know, but it really makes little difference: either way, healing comes from above. We are the ones who draw distinctions between the natural and the supernatural. All of it is God's realm. I simply feel blessed to have both available to me—friends on praying knees as well as doctors with skilled hands.

One positive aspect of medical solutions is that they get us involved. Becoming active agents of God in our own healing process builds our faith by giving us hope. Following the recommendations of my caring and committed doctors was a powerful encouragement to me. I have complete faith that God led me to those specific doctors, and I thank God for them every day.

When we face a serious disease, the first thing we should do is talk to God. Ask Him for guidance, and then take advantage of the best medical assistance available, as Hezekiah did. Ultimately, our God is *Jehovah-Rophe*—"the LORD who heals you" (Exodus 15:26)—whether He heals us with a miracle, with medicines, or in the world to come.

The Praise

Hezekiah's memoir of his experience with disease continues in Isaiah 38:17-20, where he records a testimony of praise to the God who healed him:

> *It was for my own peace*
> *That I had great bitterness;*
> *But You have lovingly delivered my soul from the pit*
> *   of corruption,*
> *For you have cast all my sins behind Your back. . . .*

The Lord was ready to save me;
Therefore we will sing my songs with stringed instruments
All the days of our life, in the house of the Lord.

ISAIAH 38:17, 20

Hezekiah gave all the credit to God for the miracle of healing. I can't read his memoir without being reminded of this psalm:

Bless the Lord, O my soul;
And all that is within me, bless His holy name!
Bless the Lord, O my soul,
And forget not all His benefits:
Who forgives all your iniquities,
Who heals all your diseases.

PSALM 103:1-3

This passage reminds us that upon recovering from illness, our first order of business should be to praise God. Some people never think of such a thing; they pray in the time of peril and quickly forget God when they are healed. Do you see a lack of consistency here—or worse, a lack of gratitude? If we pray for healing, why wouldn't we thank God when healing comes?

Are some illnesses so small and insignificant that we shouldn't bother God with them? Absolutely not! It's common for people to thank God when they've experienced a close brush with death, as in a barely missed traffic collision, but far too few of us praise Him after getting over the flu or a migraine headache. If we can pray over serious illnesses, why shouldn't we pray over *all* illnesses? Nothing that hurts us is too small for His concern.

In fact, Scripture teaches us to pray not just about our health, but about *everything* (1 Thessalonians 5:17; Philippians 4:6-7). If we pray about everything, shouldn't we also praise God in everything (1 Thessalonians 5:18)? It's fairly simple. When can we pray? All the time. When should we praise God? Whenever we pray.

The Problem

> Hezekiah did not repay according to the favor shown him, for his heart was lifted up; therefore wrath was looming over him and over Judah and Jerusalem.
>
> 2 CHRONICLES 32:25

Unfortunately, Hezekiah's medical adventure has a tragic epilogue. After all God had done for him, after the gift of fifteen precious years added to his life span, Hezekiah lost favor with God. How did this happen? His miraculous recovery caused him to lose his near-death humility.

As the heat died down on his problems, so did his passion for God. Rather than living humbly before his Lord, his heart began to swell with pride. And he became obsessed with wealth, looking not to God but to goods.

Hezekiah's pride in his wealth led him to make the political mistake of showing off his treasury and armory to envoys from Babylon, the empire that would later defeat his nation (Isaiah 39). The king of Babylon had sent his representatives to Hezekiah, supposedly to pay their respects during his convalescence. Their true motive, however, was to curry Hezekiah's favor toward a mutual alliance against a common enemy: Assyria. This wasn't on God's agenda.

In Hezekiah's prideful strength and overconfidence, he failed to consult the Lord on these developments, and he confided state secrets to his visitors: "There was nothing in his house or in all his dominion that Hezekiah did not show them" (Isaiah 39:2). His new "allies" took careful note.

Isaiah's heart was grieved when he heard of the king's foolhardy actions. The prophet foretold God's judgment on the nation (Isaiah 39:3-7), which later came to pass when the Babylonians destroyed Jerusalem and escorted the people of Judah into seventy years of captivity. They easily looted the treasury and the Temple because they knew where all the wealth was stored. Hezekiah, who had blessed his people by turning their hearts toward God, ultimately failed them just as deeply.

When Hezekiah died, his son, Manasseh, became king at age twelve and completely reversed all the good his father had done. For half a century, Manasseh left a trail of blood, violence, idolatry, and even sorcery through his reign. His father had lovingly cleansed the Temple; the son desecrated it with a carved image of a false god. The result of his evil leadership was military invasion and the blood of children sacrificed at pagan altars. The kingdom of Judah was on the slippery slope from which it would not recover.

God had His reasons for healing Hezekiah, even though He knew the future. Yet we can't help but observe that sometimes everyone is better off when God says no. The nation paid an exorbitant price for those fifteen extra years of Hezekiah's life. As the psalmist reminds us, be careful what you pray for; you might just get it:

> He gave them their request,
> But sent leanness into their soul.
> PSALM 106:15

Our problem is that our perspective doesn't extend much further than our noses, while God's perspective is infinite. We only know that we hurt, and we want it to stop. But if we could see how our suffering fits into God's perspective, we would realize there are things worse than our present darkness. Illness may be a necessary cog in the divine plan to bring about some good. Sometimes it is only through pain that we become who God wants us to be.

Charles H. Spurgeon, in his wry way, once declared, "I daresay the greatest earthly blessing that God can give to any of us is health, *with the exception of sickness.*"[7]

Instead of quickly pleading for deliverance, we might more wisely ask God about the purpose of our sufferings. *How can I grow through this, Lord?* We please Him deeply when we pray as Jesus did: "Nevertheless not My will, but Yours, be done" (Luke 22:42).

Practical Encouragements When Facing Disease

If a sadder but wiser Hezekiah could join us for questions and answers today, what advice might he give that would help us deal with disease? Let me suggest five possibilities.

Center Your Mind

> God has not given us a spirit of fear, but of power and of love and of a sound mind.
>
> 2 TIMOTHY 1:7

The human imagination is a powerful force that can create beautiful visions of a desirable future or conjure up every worst-case scenario. These dark products of the imagination can put us in the grip of fear—a place God would never have us go. As this Scripture verse shows, the power that banishes fear is a sound mind.

We maintain a sound mind by "bringing every thought into captivity to the obedience of Christ" (2 Corinthians 10:5). Paul wrote those words when false apostles in Corinth were spreading lies about his ministry. When a thought that is not from God enters our heads ("I'm sick; I'm going to die!"), we examine it in light of "the knowledge of God" (verse 5). Does this thought have any basis in reality? If not, we take it captive. No longer can it run free and lead our imaginations away from God's goodness and into unhealthy fear.

When Isobel Kuhn was fighting cancer, she realized that the real enemy was something too deep for the surgeon's scalpel. It lay in the invisible world of her imagination. She wrote,

> I had to refuse to allow my imagination to play with my future. That future, I believe, is ordered of God, and no man can guess it. For me to let myself imagine how or when the end would come was not only unprofitable, it was definitely harmful, so I had to bring my thoughts into captivity that they might not dishonor Christ.[8]

How different would your life be if you could simply take your thoughts captive for Christ? How much better would you sleep at night? How much happier and less anxious would you be? How much more joyful would friends find you?

Gaining a sound and centered mind is not as difficult as you think. If we simply read the Scriptures deeply, thoughtfully, and openly every day, we will invite the Holy Spirit to whisper new strength into our thoughts. He and He alone can tame the reckless power of the human mind. A mind centered on the truth of God is the key to being sustained and not losing heart.

Count Your Blessings

> *In everything give thanks; for this is the will of God in*
> *Christ Jesus for you.*
>
> 1 THESSALONIANS 5:18

What would you think if you opened your Bible to Ephesians 1 and read, "Blessed be the God and Father of our Lord Jesus Christ, who, *when we are well and healthy,* has blessed us with every spiritual blessing in the heavenly places in Christ" (verse 3)?

You probably know that the italicized words I inserted in that verse are nowhere to be found in Ephesians or anywhere else in the Bible. God has blessed us with every spiritual blessing in the heavenly places in Christ—period! Whether we are strong or weak, sound of body or wracked with pain, we are blessed. "From the fullness of his grace we have all received one blessing after another" (John 1:16, NIV).

You may wonder how in the midst of debilitating illness we can possibly feel blessed. It's not a matter just of feeling blessed, as if it is something we must conjure up from our imaginations; it is a matter of seeing the enormous blessings that are truly there. In her book *Gold by Moonlight,* Amy Carmichael compares living with pain and disease to a hike through a rugged terrain. Even a bleak landscape, she observes, has cheering surprises, like "bright flowers of the edelweiss waiting to be gathered among the rough rocks of difficult circumstances."[9]

In times of sickness, our blessings become clearer, richer,

and more meaningful. Something therapeutic happens deep in our hearts when we count those blessings. We can rejoice in the prayers of our friends, in a note from a loved one, in the compassionate care of a conscientious nurse, in the smile of a doctor, in the verse of a hymn that comes to mind, in a neighbor who mows the lawn, in a Bible verse that shows up at just the right time, in a prescription that lessens our pain, in a column of sunlight that cuts through the window of the room, in the intricate design of a flower in a nearby vase, or in the innocence and cheer of a grandchild who visits us. In sickness, our focus sharpens, and our perception of what's truly important narrows to exclude the peripheral values that clutter our lives when good health keeps us too busy to appreciate the simple blessings, which are often the best ones.

Training ourselves to spot these "wildflowers in the wilderness" is the secret to learning to "count it all joy" (James 1:2). This may not be easy, but it is essential to maintaining our spiritual and attitudinal health. It frees us from the tyranny of being limited to a deteriorating physical frame. It's liberating to realize that disease does not define who we are—that we are more than our aches and pains.

Illness also leads us to shift our focus in another way— from the earthly to the heavenly. This is a vital shift that can play an important part in our eventual healing.

Dr. Ed Dobson was senior pastor of Calvary Church in Grand Rapids, Michigan, when he was diagnosed with ALS (Lou Gehrig's disease)—a degenerative and terminal illness. For several years he tried to maintain his pastoral ministry with the earnest support of his church. When it became obvious that he couldn't continue, he stepped out of his pastoral role with great reluctance.

But nothing could stop Ed from continuing to bless the Lord in all things and to develop the disciplines of praise and personal worship. Ed and his oldest son had once taken a course in Judaism at a local synagogue, where they'd learned the traditional Jewish blessing that begins, "Blessed are you God our God, King of the universe. . . ." Dobson wrote,

> In the midst of my disease, I began blessing God for all the gifts of life. I use this official formula (I learned to do it in Hebrew), and I bless God for each day. I bless God for the ability to shower and clothe myself. I bless God for the ability to button buttons. I bless God for the ability to lift food to my mouth even though I can no longer do it with my right hand. I bless God for everything I can do and for every gift that comes from Him.[10]

It is always good spiritual arithmetic. If we ask God for a calm, thankful heart that sees all the blessings His grace imparts, He can teach us many lessons in illness that can never be learned in health. As the old Puritan preacher Thomas Watson put it, "A sick-bed often teaches more than a sermon."[11]

The Bible doesn't say we have to be thankful *for* all things, like the pain and discomfort of illness. But it does say we should give thanks *in* all things—including illness: "In every thing give thanks: for this is the will of God in Christ Jesus concerning you" (1 Thessalonians 5:18, KJV). Be thankful that even your sickness gives you an opportunity to glorify God.

Continue Your Work

We are His workmanship, created in Christ Jesus for good works, which God prepared beforehand that we should walk in them.

EPHESIANS 2:10

Many Christians know how God saved them—by grace through faith—but not all know *why* God saved them: "for good works, which God prepared beforehand that we should walk in them" (Ephesians 2:10). And as the great NBA star and Hall of Famer Jerry West once said, "You can't get much done in life if you only work on the days when you feel good."

As long as we're on this earth, there is work we can do. Even when we can't walk in the body, we can walk in the Spirit. On his deathbed, the prophet Elisha continued to counsel Joash, the king of Israel (2 Kings 13:14). History is filled with examples of saints who served God as long as body and breath would allow.

As Isobel Kuhn battled cancer, she discovered that staying busy was good medicine for her. Though largely confined to bed, she drew up a daily schedule that fit within the limits of her strength. She worked on her book, engaged in a ministry of prayer, read, studied, and rejoiced in letters and cards that came from all over the world.

When she lacked the strength even for these activities, she wrote, "Sound health and a normal life I cannot have while on this platform. Therefore I accept the fact and do not fret about it."[12]

Isobel Kuhn passed away on March 20, 1957, full of faith and joy. "Facing the end of one's earthly pilgrimage is not a melancholy thing for a Christian," she wrote. "It is like preparation for the most exciting journey of all. . . . And so the platform of a dreaded disease becomes but a springboard for heaven."[13]

The Englishman John Pounds (1766–1839) is another example of someone who faced illness faithfully. He was a tall, muscular, teenage laborer at the docks of Portsmouth who fell from the top of a ship's mast.

When workers reached him, he was nothing but a mass of broken bones. For two years he lay in bed as his bones healed crookedly. His pain never ceased. Out of boredom, he began to read the Bible.

Eventually, John crawled from bed, hoping to find something he could do with his life. A shoemaker hired him, and day after day, John sat at his cobbler's bench, a Bible open on his lap. Soon he was born again through faith in Christ. John gathered enough money to purchase his own little shoe shop, where he developed a pair of orthopedic boots for his crippled nephew. Soon he was making corrective shoes for other children, and his cobbler's shop became a miniature children's hospital.

As John's burden for children grew, he began feeding homeless children, teaching them to read and telling them about the Lord. His shop became known as "the Ragged School." John often limped around the waterfront with food in his pocket, looking for more children to tend. John Pounds rescued five hundred children from despair and led every one of them to Christ. His work became so famous that a Ragged School movement swept England. In John's honor, Parliament passed a series of laws to establish schools for poor children— boys' homes, girls' homes, day schools, and evening schools. All had Bible classes in which thousands heard the Gospel.

John collapsed and died on New Year's Day in 1839 while tending a boy's ulcerated foot. He was buried in a churchyard on High Street. All of England mourned, and in the church was hung a tablet that reads, "Thou shalt be blessed, for they could not recompense thee."[14]

What might John Pounds have become had he not been severely injured? We don't know. But we do know what he became in spite of his injury—or perhaps because of it. It's an inspiring reminder that our afflictions and limitations don't mean God is finished with us. The weaker we become, the more God's grace is multiplied (2 Corinthians 12:9). Going through a rough patch often equips us for further service. It also allows us to empathize with and minister to people who otherwise would never have crossed our paths.

We would discard suffering as a vile thing, but God wastes nothing. In His hands, suffering becomes the means for miracles. He will open new doors of witness, and His strength will shine through our weaknesses.

Claim Your Promises

[Jesus said,] "This sickness is not unto death, but for the glory of God, that the Son of God may be glorified through it."

JOHN 11:4

I said earlier that healing has a dual purpose—our good and God's glory. Jesus went a step further when He said that even death can glorify God.

Perhaps the greatest truth in the entire Bible as it relates to sickness among Christians comes from the words of Jesus in John 11:4. His friend Lazarus was ill and went on to die, and when Jesus arrived, His friend had been in the tomb four days. But Jesus didn't say that Lazarus's sickness wouldn't *include* death. He said that it wouldn't *end* in death. It would provide instead an occasion for God to be glorified.

Because of the resurrection of Jesus Christ, we must cling with hope to the promise that, although our illnesses may include death, they will not end in death; we, too, will be resurrected. Armed with this truth, we can see how God can glorify Himself even through disease. And when we are faced with life-threatening sickness, our fear can be replaced by a determination to glorify the One who "works all things according to the counsel of His will" (Ephesians 1:11).

Consider Your Future

I consider that the sufferings of this present time are not worthy to be compared with the glory which shall be revealed in us.

ROMANS 8:18

Suppose you won a free trip around the world for you and a loved one. It included first-class accommodations at five-star hotels, private planes, lavish gifts, and personal tours. (See how powerful the imagination is?) But suppose as you opened the envelope containing the tickets, you suffered a paper cut on the end of your finger. You might say to your companion, "Oh, I cut my finger!" You'd grimace for about half a second before grinning from ear to ear and saying, "Who cares? We're about to take the trip of a lifetime!"

I would say nothing to trivialize disease; I know the misery of it firsthand. But according to Paul, and from the perspective of our eternal God, the sufferings of this present world are less than a paper cut in relation to the glory yet to be revealed to us.

Although Christ has conquered sin and death, the

effects of both linger. But only temporarily. Disease must be accepted, but only for now—and always with the knowledge that its master, death itself, no longer has power over us. If this life were all we had, then cancer and every other life-threatening illness would truly be tragic. But because death's prison doors have been destroyed, death can no longer hold us captive. This is why Paul says, "To live is Christ, and to die is gain" (Philippians 1:21). We look forward to our new resurrection bodies, perfect and free from all defects. As Paul explains, Christ will "transform our lowly body that it may be conformed to His glorious body, according to the working by which He is able even to subdue all things to Himself" (Philippians 3:21).

It would be nice to be healed here and now, as Lazarus and Hezekiah were. But if not, we'll simply be healed later. Every one of us who belongs to Jesus Christ holds a Lazarus coupon. What Jesus did for him, God will do for us. The big difference is that our restored lives will be eternally free from further disease. "God will wipe away every tear from [our] eyes; there shall be no more death, nor sorrow, nor crying. There shall be no more pain, for the former things have passed away" (Revelation 21:4).

Dr. Jonathan Thigpen, former president of the Evangelical Training Association, was forty-five years old when he began having some muscular disorders. The diagnosis was the same as that of Ed Dobson—ALS, or Lou Gehrig's disease. This disease is debilitating and terminal: it has no known cause or cure.

Thigpen describes the chilling fear he felt after learning of his diagnosis: "I remember walking out of the doctor's office in Carol Stream, Illinois, and deep in the pit of my stomach there was a feeling of overwhelming fear. . . . It felt like I was being hugged by something so dark and so horrible that I can't describe it."[15]

Then an old, familiar voice echoed through his memory—the voice of his father, Dr. Charles Thigpen, reading the words of Psalm 46:

> God is our refuge and strength, a very present help
> in trouble.
> Therefore we will not fear,
> Even though the earth be removed,
> And though the mountains be carried into the midst
> of the sea;
> Though its waters roar and be troubled,
> Though the mountains shake with its swelling.
> PSALM 46:1-3

Many times Jonathan had tagged along as his dad visited hospital patients and read those soothing and powerful words. Now it was his own soul that was soothed. As he reached his car, the dark clouds overshadowing his spirit began to dissipate. God was still in control—he knew it for a certainty. Jonathan didn't have any answers, but he knew that "fear cannot stand in the face of a faith and a God who does not change. My fear had left."[16]

Jonathan took hold of Psalm 46 as so many of us often do with particular Scripture passages that hold remarkable power just when we need it. In the months that followed, Jonathan's spirit was willing but his flesh was increasingly weak as he traveled the country sharing those words about his refuge and his strength, the help he had found to be very present in his time of trouble. Once again, Christ claimed victory in the face of what had seemed a meaningless misfortune.

A Puritan preacher once wrote, "Sickness, when sanctified, teaches us four things: the vanity of the world, the vileness of sin, the helplessness of man and the preciousness of Christ."[17] The last of those, I submit, overpowers the emptiness of the others. If heaven is what lies ahead for us, what can we possibly complain about?

Instead, think of the best: we have a Great Physician who raised His own Son from the dead, leaving behind an empty tomb. We have a heavenly home with welcoming doors opened wide. We have a sympathetic Savior who never imparts a spirit of fear but a spirit of power, love, and a sound mind. To understand that is to enjoy a spiritual health that overcomes the darkest days that disease can inflict.

CHAPTER 5

HOPE WHEN FACING DISASTER

We will not fear, even though the earth be removed,
and though the mountains be carried into the midst of the sea.

PSALM 46:2

At least the Trowbridges had a place to hide—a neighbor's cellar. Kelcy, her husband, and their three children filed into its cool darkness, huddled beneath a blanket, and listened to the warning sirens howling through a Monday afternoon in May of 2013. The Trowbridges lived in the suburbs of Oklahoma City, and a deadly tornado was on its way.

The family could only sit, holding hands and listening as the sirens were drowned out by sounds that were louder and far more terrible. Shrieking winds converged upon the house, and there was a violent pounding on the cellar door. The children began to cry. "Shhh, it's just debris," Kelcy said. "Loose things blowing around, hitting the walls."

Then, after about forty minutes, an eerie silence fell. The Trowbridges emerged into the light of a world they didn't recognize. The neighborhood was a shambles. Where was their home? It lay flattened to the earth, like rows of other houses on their street. Where was the family car? They eventually discovered that it had been lifted into the air, carried down the street, and then thrown on its roof.

One by one, the neighbors emerged, all speechless. Where there should have been birds singing, there was only the sound of muffled sobs. Here were the remains of their lives and the loss of comfortable illusions—illusions of stability and security in a rational world.

Mr. Trowbridge wasn't one to stand around. He went to work salvaging, sorting. But after a moment, he pulled back abruptly.

"Call the police," he said in a flat tone.

There, amid the bricks and pipes and rubble, was a little child—a girl no more than two or three years old. She was dead. Mr. Trowbridge was stoic until the police arrived, and then he lost it—weeping for the girl, for his family, for the violence of the earth.

Meanwhile, near Plaza Towers Elementary, Stuart Earnest Jr. saw and heard things that he knew would haunt him for the rest of his life. The school was directly hit by the tornado. Seven children lost their lives, and Earnest couldn't block out the sounds of the tragedy. He heard the voices of those screaming for help and the equally heartrending screams of those trying to come to their assistance.

A fourth grader named Damian Britton was among the Plaza Towers survivors, thanks to a courageous teacher who had saved his life. It seemed to Damian that all the horrors occurred in a five-minute period before the students came out of their hiding places.

It was much the same everywhere—five short minutes for little ones, or anyone else, to learn such profound lessons of life and loss.

I have to tell you that it is difficult to recount those stories. It would be so much easier to keep the tone pleasant and comfortable, even in a book like this one. The problem, of course, is that the stories are true, and we know it. And they can happen again in another five minutes or tomorrow or the next day. Every year the news brings us yet another reminder that the natural forces governing this planet are troubled and unstable.

We live in a kind of necessary denial. We proceed with our daily lives as if we have guarantees of security that simply aren't possible in this life. We congratulate ourselves for our impressive advances in technology, and we pretend we've conquered every challenge to life and health. But it's not so. Nature is gorgeous and inspiring—and also monstrous and inhuman.

There are too many earthquakes, fires, floods, hurricanes, tornadoes, famines, storms, and tsunamis for us to even keep a running tally. Natural calamities rage on in our world, costing us countless billions of dollars and, more significantly, hundreds of thousands of lives.

Natural disaster raises many questions about the nature of our security, about our fear of the uncontrollable, and especially about the character of God. These questions need answers. But I'd like to open the discussion by sharing about a biblical character who experienced two natural disasters in the space of twenty-four hours. His name, of course, was Job.

Natural Disasters in the Life of Job

Job has become the quintessential model for enduring disaster, and if ever there was someone we'd think didn't deserve it, it was Job. The first few verses of his book give testimony concerning Job in four areas. We learn first of all about his *faith*—that he was a man who was "blameless and upright, and one who feared God and shunned evil" (Job 1:1). Job was not sinless, but he was mature in character and a man of righteousness.

Job is also distinguished because of his *fortune*: "His possessions were seven thousand sheep, three thousand camels, five hundred yoke of oxen, five hundred female donkeys, and a very large household, so that this man was the greatest of all the people of the East" (Job 1:3).

In Job's day, wealth was calculated in terms of land, animals, and servants, and Job had all three in abundance. He was the wealthiest man of his time.

He wasn't just a man of fortune but also of *family*. The first chapter tells us that he raised sons and daughters who were close knit. They held great birthday feasts for one another, after which their father would make burnt offerings to God on their behalf. He said, "It may be that my sons have sinned and cursed God in their hearts" (Job 1:5). Faith and family were intertwined for him.

Finally, he had many *friends*. Some are famous for their role in Job's book, but there were no doubt many others who weren't mentioned. Job 2:11 recounts how a group of his closest friends arrived to mourn with him after the great losses he sustained. If you know anything about Job's narrative, you remember that these friends ended up letting him down. But still, they were his friends, and they came from distant parts to minister to him in his time of need.

They were right to sit with him to help him bear the load of mourning. Where they went wrong was when they attempted to give pat explanations and solutions for a situation that was anything but simple. In the end, they brought out the worst rather than the best in Job. Yet we're told that he forgave them and there was reconciliation (Job 42:9-11).

What those friends couldn't know—what Job himself couldn't know—was that spiritual forces were in play far beyond their reckoning. The details are recounted in Job 1:8-12:

> The LORD said to Satan, "Have you considered My
> servant Job, that there is none like him on the earth,
> a blameless and upright man, one who fears God and
> shuns evil?"

So Satan answered the LORD and said, "Does Job fear God for nothing? Have You not made a hedge around him, around his household, and around all that he has on every side? You have blessed the work of his hands, and his possessions have increased in the land. But now, stretch out Your hand and touch all that he has, and he will surely curse You to Your face!"

And the LORD said to Satan, "Behold, all that he has is in your power; only do not lay a hand on his person." So Satan went out from the presence of the LORD.

Armed with God's permission, Satan went to work, and Job's ruin came rapidly, with four calamities occurring in one day. These were the terms: Satan could come after Job's possessions, but not his person. And so the great experiment began. But what we see already is that it's clear who is in charge of this world. The devil can test Job, but not without God's permission. Our God reigns, and we can't afford to forget it during a discussion of disaster—or any other time.

What do you give the man who has everything? Disaster— that was something Job had yet to experience. It begins during one of those feasts, with the sons and daughters all gathered together, laughing and enjoying one another's company.

A messenger approaches Job with disturbing news. Sabean raiders have descended on his estate, hijacked Job's cattle, and killed his servants. This messenger alone has survived to tell the tale (Job 1:13-15).

Yet even before the servant has finished his account, before Job has taken it all in, the door opens and another messenger stands there. He is pale, his eyes wide, as he whispers, "The fire of God fell from heaven and burned up the sheep and the servants" (Job 1:16).

At this point it seems that Job's day can't get any worse. But a third messenger is right behind. The phrase "while he was still speaking" is used three times in this passage. For Job, at least, the old adage is true: calamities often come in bunches.

The third messenger brings news that there has been a raid by the Chaldeans. They have stolen the camels, killed the servants, and yes, left one distressed messenger (Job 1:17).

A lot has gone wrong for Job—calamity piled upon calamity. But before he can make sense of any of this, let alone form any kind of recovery plan, the coup de grâce falls:

> While he was still speaking, another also came and said,
> "Your sons and daughters were eating and drinking wine
> in their oldest brother's house, and suddenly a great wind
> came from across the wilderness and struck the four
> corners of the house, and it fell on the young people, and
> they are dead; and I alone have escaped to tell you!"
> JOB 1:18-19

Along with everything else, Job must have been blessed with a strong heart. Can you imagine taking in such news? He was devoted to his children, constantly bringing them before God. Despite all his intercession, they have died in one fell blow. He faces ten fresh graves and an aching silence from heaven. *Why, God?*

The book of Job has always been the go-to book to help people cope with the existence and effects of evil. At the outset, the book shows us three major sources of evil. First, there are evil individuals, such as the Sabeans and the Chaldeans who killed Job's servants and stole his oxen and donkeys. Then it shows the destructive evil of natural disasters in the fire that destroyed Job's livestock and herders and the windstorm that killed Job's children. And behind it all, we see evil on a cosmic level in the hand of Satan who, with God's permission, orchestrated the entire disaster.

Since scholars consider Job to be the oldest book in the Bible, we know that the problem of natural disasters has been with us for as long as human beings have walked the earth. The Bible doesn't gloss over the tougher questions of life; it doesn't try to make us avert our gaze. We're invited to stand with Job in the cemetery, looking down at the ashes of his dreams, and ask God *why?* The first question evoked by this story in particular and natural calamities in general is this: What do these recurring disasters say about God?

Natural Disasters and the Reality of God

God Cannot Be Divorced from Disasters

Some say that God should not even be included in the discussion of disasters since He would have nothing to do with such evil. The explanation goes something like this: God created the world, but He is not involved in the operation of it. This philosophy is called deism. It accepts the existence and goodness of God but distances Him from anything that happens in the world He created.

I think many Christians adopt a sort of deism in an attempt to get God off the hook. It allows us to affirm the goodness of God in the face of terrible evils simply by saying it's not His fault. He created a good world, and He should not be blamed if it goes wrong. But Scripture is clear that God is actively at work in the universe (Job 37).

Another way we extricate God from responsibility for disasters is to blame them all on Satan. But we know from our study of Job that Satan cannot do anything without God's permission (Job 1:8-12). If Satan has to get permission from God to do what he does, then God is still in control and reigns in human affairs. People sense His control over everything when they call natural disasters "acts of God."

So for us to say that God is not involved in these cataclysmic events is too simplistic to explain all the facts. Whether it's comfortable or not, we must discuss this issue with theological integrity. The Bible teaches us that God is sovereign— He reigns in the nice moments and in those that aren't so nice. Let's look at some of the reasons disaster exists in a world that God controls.

GOD EMPLOYS THE ELEMENTS OF NATURE IN THE OPERATION OF THE WORLD

The Bible contains many passages refuting the idea that God set nature in motion and now lets it run as it will. These

Scriptures present a hands-on God who is intimately involved in controlling and sustaining all events in the natural world. Here is a small sampling:

Whatever the LORD *pleases He does,*
In heaven and in earth,
In the seas and in all deep places.
He causes the vapors to ascend from
the ends of the earth;
He makes lightning for the rain;
He brings the wind out of His treasuries.

PSALM 135:6-7

He makes His sun rise on the evil and on the good, and
sends rain on the just and on the unjust.

MATTHEW 5:45

He says to the snow, "Fall on the earth";
Likewise to the gentle rain and the heavy rain of His
      strength. . . .
By the breath of God ice is given,
And the broad waters are frozen.
Also with moisture He saturates the thick clouds;
He scatters His bright clouds.
And they swirl about, being turned by His guidance,
That they may do whatever He commands them
On the face of the whole earth.

JOB 37:6, 10-12

GOD EMPLOYS THE ELEMENTS OF NATURE IN HIS OPPOSITION TO EVIL

Not only does God use the elements of nature to keep the world running, He also uses them as punishment or to drive His people toward righteousness.

Early in the Bible, we find God sending a flood to destroy a sin-blackened world, sparing only righteous Noah and his family (Genesis 6–8). Later, when the Israelites were wandering in the desert, God sent judgment upon Dathan, Abiram, and Korah, who had rejected Him. The "earth opened its mouth and swallowed them up . . . with all their goods" (Numbers 16:32).

God sent fire to destroy Sodom and Gomorrah because of their wickedness (Genesis 19:24); He sent plagues to punish Egypt (Exodus 7–12); He crafted a plague that killed seventy thousand men because of David's sin in numbering the people (2 Samuel 24:15); He sent a fierce storm to get Jonah's attention and bring him to repentance (Jonah 1:4-17).

In Amos 4, there is an extended passage describing God's dealings with the disobedience of His people. If we're ever tempted to separate God from natural disaster, this passage should stop us in our tracks. Here is Eugene Peterson's vivid paraphrase:

> "You know, don't you, that I'm the One
>   who emptied your pantries and cleaned out your
>   cupboards,

Who left you hungry and standing in bread lines?
  But you never got hungry for me. You continued to
    ignore me."
  GOD's Decree.

"Yes, and I'm the One who stopped the rains
    three months short of harvest.
I'd make it rain on one village
    but not on another.
I'd make it rain on one field
    but not on another—and that one would dry up.
People would stagger from village to village
    crazed for water and never quenching their thirst.
But you never got thirsty for me.
    You ignored me."
  GOD's Decree.

"I hit your crops with disease
    and withered your orchards and gardens.
Locusts devoured your olive and fig trees,
    but you continued to ignore me."
  GOD's Decree.

"I revisited you with the old Egyptian plagues,
    killed your choice young men and prize horses.
The stink of rot in your camps was so strong
    that you held your noses—
But you didn't notice me.

You continued to ignore me."
GOD's *Decree.*

"I hit you with earthquake and fire,
      left you devastated like Sodom and Gomorrah.
You were like a burning stick
      snatched from the flames.
But you never looked my way.
      You continued to ignore me."
          GOD's *Decree.*

AMOS 4:6-11, *THE MESSAGE*

When we distance God from responsibility for the calamities of the world, we are claiming more than we know. For if God is not in control of the world's disasters, then how can we depend on Him to be in control of our lives and the future? Either He is involved in all the world's operations, or He's involved in none of them.

Before we move on, it is critical that I make a distinction between God's general judgment on the sin of humankind and His supposed judgment on the sin of particular men and women. It is true to say that all God's judgment is because of sin and that He uses disasters in administering judgment. But it is not true to say that every particular disaster is His judgment of some particular sin committed by some particular person or nation.

After 9/11, some people were quick to point out that the disaster was God's judgment on our nation for our rebellion against Him. While that may have been true, how would anyone on earth know for sure?

Almost all the disasters and tragedies that have befallen our nation in the last several years have incited some pundit to declare the tragedy a particular judgment for a particular sin that had been committed in the immediate context of the disaster. The truth is, we don't know the mysteries of God's heart and will. In Luke's Gospel, Jesus warns against playing the armchair prophet. Pilate had murdered some Galileans, and others had been killed when a tower collapsed at Siloam. When asked about it, Jesus said,

> Do you suppose that these Galileans were worse sinners than all other Galileans, because they suffered such things? I tell you, no; but unless you repent you will all likewise perish. Or those eighteen on whom the tower in Siloam fell and killed them, do you think that they were worse sinners than all other men who dwelt in Jerusalem? I tell you, no; but unless you repent you will all likewise perish.
>
> LUKE 13:2-5

Jesus was reminding us that in our fallen world, disasters happen, and they happen to both evil and righteous people without distinction or explanation. It's not up to us to label this one as misfortune or that one as God's judgment but simply, as Jesus pointed out, to ponder the sin in our own hearts.

God Cannot Be Discredited by Disasters

Some people, of course, remove God from the equation entirely; He simply doesn't exist, they argue, and disasters are all the proof we need.

Atheist George Smith speaks for those who would attempt to make this case with tidy logic: "The problem of evil is this. . . . If God knows there is evil but cannot prevent it, he is not omnipotent. If God knows there is evil and can prevent it but desires not to, he is not omnibenevolent."[1]

Sometimes it is sheer emotion rather than cut-and-dried reasoning that provokes such a conclusion. After the 2010 tsunami, a commentator in Scotland's newspaper *The Herald* wrote,

> God, if there is a God, should be ashamed of Himself. The sheer enormity of the Asian tsunami disaster, the death, destruction, and havoc it has wreaked, the scale of misery it has caused, must surely test the faith of even the firmest believer. . . . I hope I am right . . . that there is no God. For if there were, then He'd have to shoulder the blame. In my book, He would be as guilty as sin and I'd want nothing to do with Him.[2]

But wait a minute—not so fast. C. S. Lewis, once an atheist himself, saw disasters not as a proof against the existence of God but, reasoning as he did when he came to faith in Christ, as actual proof of God's existence:

My argument against God was that the universe
seemed so cruel and unjust. But how had I got
this idea of *just* and *unjust*? A man does not call a
line crooked unless he has some idea of a straight
line. What was I comparing this universe with
when I called it unjust? If the whole show was bad
and senseless from A to Z, so to speak, why did
I, who was supposed to be part of the show, find
myself in violent reaction against it? . . . Thus in
the very act of trying to prove that God did not
exist—in other words, that the whole of reality was
senseless—I found I was forced to assume that one
part of reality—namely my idea of justice—was
full of sense. Consequently atheism turns out to
be too simple. If the whole of the universe has no
meaning, we should never have found out that it
has no meaning: just as, if there were no light in
the universe and therefore no creatures with eyes,
we should never know it was dark. *Dark* would
be without meaning.[3]

The fact that we have a strong idea of justice and perfection in a world contaminated with injustice and imperfection
gives compelling evidence that a good God does exist.

One truth we often overlook is that massive deaths caused
by disaster cannot discredit God any more than a single death
can. We know who brought death into the world, and it
wasn't God. We must remember that every one of the people

who died in the Haiti earthquake would eventually have died anyway. The fact that they died simultaneously is really no more tragic than if their deaths had been spread out over the next several decades. It's just that the sudden and unexpected simultaneous deaths shock us more.

God Cannot Be Defined by Disasters

In the aftermath of every disaster, we often hear something like this: "I could never believe in a God who would allow such awful things to happen to His creatures."

The God these people want to believe in is the "helicopter parent" God who hovers just above us at all times, insulating us from all unpleasantness like an overprotective father. They want a God who guarantees safety, security, and happiness and spares us from all tragedy and pain, even disciplinary pain. God is better than that. He does not indulge our every desire but rather administers discipline to help us become the kind of creatures who can inhabit a blissful eternity.

Those who define God solely by the evil He allows overlook the flip side of their complaint. Yes, there is evil in the world, but there is also an enormous amount of good. If God is not good, as they claim, how do they account for all the good we experience? Is it fair to judge Him for the evil and not credit Him with the good?

In his book *Where Was God?* Erwin Lutzer writes,

Often the same people who ask where God was following a disaster thanklessly refuse to worship and honor Him for years of peace and calmness. They disregard God in good times, yet think He is obligated to provide help when bad times come. They believe the God they dishonor when they are well should heal them when they are sick; the God they ignore when they are wealthy should rescue them from impending poverty; and the God they refuse to worship when the earth is still should rescue them when it begins to shake.

We must admit that God owes us nothing. Before we charge God with not caring, we must thank Him for those times when His care is very evident. We are ever surrounded by undeserved blessings. Even in His silence, He blesses us.[4]

In a world that contains tragedies, we must realize that they're vastly outnumbered by blessings. A little clear thinking underlines the point that we can't allow others to define God for us. The Bible and good common sense erase a lot of confusion.

There's no denying that we live in a world where many bad things happen, and much of it seems undeserved. "Why do bad things happen to good people?" Apologist Dinesh D'Souza asks. "The Christian answer is that there are no good people. None of us deserves the life that we have, which is a gratuitous gift from God."[5]

God is loving, and His gifts abound in our world. So does

His discipline. That is why we must refuse to let only one side of the equation define God for us.

God Cannot Be Defeated by Disasters

When disasters happen, we are sometimes tempted to think that God's purposes have been thwarted. Let's allow God to speak for Himself on this subject:

> I am God, and there is no other;
> I am God, and there is none like Me,
> Declaring the end from the beginning,
> And from ancient times things that are not yet done,
> Saying, "My counsel shall stand,
> And I will do all My pleasure." . . .
> Indeed I have spoken it;
> I will also bring it to pass.
> I have purposed it;
> I will also do it.
>
> ISAIAH 46:9-11

One reason we fear disasters is that their occurrence makes it seem that God is not in control, that somehow things have slipped out of His grasp. At such times we must remember that a single thread in the grand tapestry cannot comprehend the pattern of the whole. Our view is too limited to perceive any ultimate meaning in a calamity—how our present suffering fits into God's ultimate purpose. Yet, as Paul tells us,

"We know that all things work together for good to those who love God, to those who are the called according to His purpose" (Romans 8:28).

Like every other piece of this entangled subject, this verse is easy to confuse in its meaning. As James Montgomery Boice tells us, Paul is not saying that evil things are good:

> The text does not teach that sickness, suffering, persecution, grief, or any other such thing is itself good. On the contrary, these things are evils. Hatred is not love. Death is not life. Grief is not joy. The world is filled with evil. But what the text teaches . . . is that God uses these things to effect his own good ends for people. God brings good out of evil.[6]

God brought good out of the work by which Satan meant to destroy Job's faith. And He used the awful reality of the crucifixion of a perfect Christ for wonderful purposes. In God's wise and powerful hands, evil events are used as tools to work toward good ends.

The clue is in the ordering of the words in the original language: "We know that for those who love God," the Greek text reads, "He is working." In other words, God is ceaselessly, energetically, and purposefully active on their behalf. He is involved; He is busy creating a glorious destiny for those who love Him.

The phrase Paul uses to describe how God works on our behalf is interesting. He says that "all things work together."

This expression is translated from the Greek word *sunergeo*, from which we get our word *synergism*. Synergism is the working together of various elements to produce an effect greater than, and often completely different from, the sum of each element acting separately.

So things do not just work out somehow if we let nature take its course. God causes this synergism to happen. He is the One who stirs the mix! This is why disaster cannot defeat God or derail His plans and purposes. All nature is under His control: *all things* work together. The One who controls nature holds us in His hands.

Donald Grey Barnhouse explains that the "we know" part of Romans 8:28 is a superb antidote to the fear of disaster:

> It is possible here and now for us to know that all things work together for our good. To lay hold of that fact is to calm the turbulence of life and to bring quiet and confidence into the whole of life. Nothing can touch me unless it passes through the will of God. God has a plan for my life. God is working according to a fixed, eternal purpose.[7]

In the following poem, Annie Johnson Flint uses the intricate workings of factory machinery to give us a creative picture of God's complete control of "all things":

> *In a factory building, there are wheels and gearings,*
> *There are cranks, pulleys, belts either tight or slack—*

Some are whirling swiftly, some are turning slowly,
Some are thrusting forward, some are pulling back;
Some are smooth and silent, some are rough and noisy,
Pounding, rattling, clanking, moving with a jerk;
In a wild confusion in a seeming chaos,
Lifting, pushing, driving—but they do their work.
From the mightiest lever to the smallest cog or gear,
All things move together for the purpose planned;
And behind the working is a mind controlling,
And a force directing, and a guiding hand.
So all things are working for the Lord's beloved;
Some things might be hurtful if alone they stood;
Some might seem to hinder; some might draw us backward;
But they work together, and they work for good,
All the thwarted longings, all the stern denials,
All the contradictions, hard to understand.
And the force that holds them, speeds them and retards them,
Stops and starts and guides them—is our Father's hand.[8]

Several years ago my wife and I were reminded of an inspiring example of one couple who trusted God's control over all things. While we were visiting Jerusalem, some friends took us to lunch at the American Colony Hotel. As we sat down to eat, we were handed a small brochure that told the story of the hotel and its restaurant.

I was shocked to discover that the hotel belonged to the family of Horatio Spafford, the man who wrote the words to my favorite Gospel hymn, "It Is Well with My Soul." I have often recounted the tragic circumstances that surrounded the writing of that song, but the brochure included facts I hadn't known. Here is that story:

In 1871, Horatio Spafford lived in the Lake View suburb of Chicago. He was a young lawyer with a wife, Anna, and four little girls. In October of that year, the whole center of the city was devastated by fire. No one is certain how the fire started, but it killed hundreds of people and destroyed whole sections of the city.

All across town, people were wandering homeless and hungry. The Spaffords were deeply involved in doing what they could to help families in distress. But it was no short-term ministry. Two years later, exhausted from their work, they planned a trip to Europe for rest. But at the last minute, business kept Horatio in town. Anna and the four girls boarded a ship and left the harbor.

Late one night during the voyage, another ship rammed the steamer, which sank within twenty minutes. One of only forty-seven who were rescued, Anna was pulled from the water, unconscious and floating on a piece of debris. But the four Spafford girls perished. Anna sent a telegram from Paris to her husband: "Saved alone. What shall I do?" She remarked to another passenger that God had given her four daughters and taken them away and that perhaps someday she would understand why.

Horatio boarded a ship to find his wife and bring her home. When the ship's path crossed the very point where his daughters had been lost, the captain called him to his cabin and told him so. Horatio, deeply moved, found a piece of paper from the hotel in which he had stayed before the voyage. He jotted down the words to "It Is Well with My Soul," now one of the world's favorite hymns.

Back in Chicago, the couple tried to start over again. A son was born to them, and then another daughter. Maybe the worst was over. But then, another tragedy: the boy died of scarlet fever at four years old.

Inexplicably, the family's church took the view that these tragedies were surely the punishment of a wrathful God for some unspecified sin on the part of the Spaffords. An elder in a church he had helped build, Horatio was asked to leave rather than being taken in and comforted by a healing community.

In 1881, the little family left the United States to begin a new life in Jerusalem. They rented a house in the Old City section, with the goal of imitating the lives of the first-century Christians as closely as possible. Soon the family was widely known for their love and service to the needy, as well as for their devotion to the Scriptures. Even today, the Spafford Children's Center serves Jerusalem and the West Bank by providing health care and educational support to as many as thirty thousand children annually under the leadership of the Spaffords' descendants.[9]

Anna and Horatio Spafford suffered severe testings of their faith, but they did not blame God for their suffering. They knew He was in control of all things, and because He could not be defeated, neither could they. Their faith allowed them to learn through their testings and to use their pain to bless others and further the Gospel.

I hope this section has helped lift the fog that obscures our understanding of God's connection with disaster. When our pain leads us to see Him as uninvolved in calamity, powerless to control it, or defeated by it, we saw off the limb that supports us, and we plunge into fear. This leaves us without hope, for an all-powerful God is our only solace in tragic times.

Now we will look at ways in which the experience of disaster can actually bless us.

Natural Disasters and the Responsibilities of Man

In the midst of pain and grief, it's hard to realize that disasters can bring vital benefits. Just as destructive forest fires clean out the underbrush that would eventually stifle the trees, disasters in our lives can cause us to see our blind spots and address them with clearer vision.

Disasters Teach Us to Repent of Our Sin

Earlier in this chapter we discussed an occasion from Luke 13 in which Jesus refers to two contemporary tragedies. Did the victims die because they were more sinful than the survivors? No, He replies; we all perish unless we repent. In other words, the greatest natural disaster of all happened in the Garden of Eden; the rest is collateral damage. The Fall makes us all victims unless we allow Jesus Christ to handle the problem of our sin.

When you read about people losing their lives in fires, floods, hurricanes, tornadoes, and tsunamis, do you ever wonder how many of them were prepared to meet their God? Does the question cause you to examine your own readiness (2 Corinthians 13:5)? Our readiness to meet God greatly reduces our fear of disaster.

Many factors are at work in the scope of a disaster, but one of them is surely the work of God drawing our attention to Himself. In truth, we are surrounded by unrecognized tragedies and disasters: a dark, sex-obsessed, violent culture; the rapid decline of morality; the deterioration of Christian influence in our world. How many more are victims to these man-made poisons than to the forces of wind and weather? Sometimes it requires the dramatic power of a hurricane or some other force in nature to capture our attention and turn our minds to matters of eternity.

God uses disasters and tragedies to accomplish His perfect will in us and through us—and sometimes to bring us to Himself in the first place. In the church I pastor, almost all who give testimony to their faith at their baptism have one thing in common: they are brought to Christ through some difficult experience. Often it is the loss of a loved one or a divorce or the loss of employment. God uses difficulty and disaster to get the attention of those He is pursuing.

How does this work? Erwin Lutzer tells us,

Disasters might drive some people away from God, but for others it has the opposite effect, driving

them into the arms of Jesus. The destruction of
nature has helped them distinguish the temporary
from the permanent. Disasters remind the living
that tomorrow is uncertain, so we must prepare for
eternity today. Today is the accepted time; today is
the day of salvation.

When disasters come, God is not on trial, *we are.*[10]

Disasters Teach Us to Reflect on God's Goodness

When I watch reports of natural disasters as they are instantaneously delivered to us through the media, my first thoughts are for the lives lost and the families torn apart. I also experience a sense of gratitude that my family and people I know were not touched by these events.

I used to feel guilty about this in the same way I felt guilty about people who got cancer at the same time I did but did not survive. But I have since come to understand that it is proper to be grateful that I have been saved even while I mourn for those who have been lost.

Mark Mittelberg writes,

It's common in the middle of a drought . . . to forget
that rain is the norm. Or in the middle of a flood
to forget that floods rarely happen. Or when bad
news comes from the doctor to forget that, for most
of us, this comes after many years of relatively good
health.[11]

God's blessings abound; they are the norm, and it's proper to be grateful for them at all times, regardless of surrounding circumstances.

Disasters Teach Us to Respond to the Hurting

The Southern California wildfires of 2003 and 2007 destroyed the homes of several of our church families and decimated a community in the mountains above our place of worship. I had never experienced anything that touched our church so directly.

To this day, people still talk about the ways they were changed for the better from an event that couldn't have seemed any worse. When the devil sends a wildfire, God sends the holy fire of Spirit-filled followers of Christ. When the devil sends a flood, God sends the refreshment of living water.

During those tragic events, many of our people did exactly what Job's friends did at first: they sat with hurting people. Sometimes silent presence is the most powerful ministry. When folks are grieving, for example, spiritual rationalizations and the wholesale quoting of Scripture verses can fall flat. People don't need our answers—they simply need our shoulders to cry on, our company in the darkness. These are the moments when the church of Jesus Christ is at its very best. And when someone finally turns to us and asks why, we can say, "I'd love to sit down with you over coffee and work on those questions together soon. But right now, I'm here to serve you. What can I do?"

In 1940, C. S. Lewis published his first popular book on

Christian doctrine, *The Problem of Pain*. It was an intellectual attack on the view that suffering and evil rule out the existence of God. It was a book for the mind—and a good one. But it didn't really touch the heart; that came twenty-one years later, when Lewis found himself writing a very different kind of book.

In *A Grief Observed*, Lewis's aching sadness and even anger radiated from every page. He had lost his beloved wife to bone cancer, and he was overwhelmed with sorrow. He was no longer interested in debating points; now his heart was broken. This new book held more questions than answers. It read as a journey of mourning that somehow arrived at a safe harbor for faith.

When he finished writing, Lewis understood that the world had never seen him this raw and emotional. He decided to publish *A Grief Observed* under the pen name N. W. Clerk. Yet soon an army of loving friends were bringing him "Clerk's" book, saying, "Here, perhaps this little volume will help you." Lewis had to come out from behind his pseudonym and admit that he was the book's author and the owner of the pain it displayed. It was the book born out of pain, even more than the book with the intellectual answers, that ministered to others who were suffering.[12]

Disasters perform a painful surgery in our inmost parts, but the Physician's hand is tender and sure. He wants to make us better, stronger, more capable of ministry in a world of broken hearts. As we minister to our own pain and the pain of others, we take on a growing resemblance to the Savior who healed pain everywhere He encountered it.

Disasters Teach Us to Remember God's Promise

God has given us a spectacular, all-encompassing promise that provides the ultimate cure for our fear of disaster. Revelation 21:3-4 says, "I heard a loud voice from heaven saying, 'Behold, the tabernacle of God is with men, and He will dwell with them, and they shall be His people. God Himself will be with them and be their God. And God will wipe away every tear from their eyes; there shall be no more death, nor sorrow, nor crying. There shall be no more pain, for the former things have passed away.'"

Disasters remind us that God doesn't intend for this fallen earth, with its death, disaster, and corruption, to be our permanent home. As the old spiritual says, "This world is not my home; I'm just a passin' through." The calamities we experience here are only temporary phenomena. Each disaster reminds us that a disaster-free eternity awaits us and inspires our hearts to hope for it.

Paul affirms this longing: "The earnest expectation of the creation eagerly waits for the revealing of the sons of God. . . . For we know that the whole creation groans and labors with birth pangs together until now" (Romans 8:19, 22).

Disasters Teach Us to Rely on God's Presence and His Power

We began this chapter by looking into the terrible experience of a man named Job. It's fitting that we return to his life again to discover how the tragic events of his life fully played themselves out.

Job experiences severe depression as he struggles to deal with his losses. But soon he finds within himself a powerful hope, a trusting commitment to God. "Though He slay me," Job resolves, "yet will I trust Him" (Job 13:15).

By the grace of God, Job manages to maintain his strong faith and reliance on God, certain that something better is in store for him:

> *I know that my Redeemer lives,*
> *And He shall stand at last on the earth;*
> *And after my skin is destroyed, this I know,*
> *That in my flesh I shall see God,*
> *Whom I shall see for myself,*
> *And my eyes shall behold, and not another.*
> *How my heart yearns within me!*
> JOB 19:25-27

Finally God speaks to Job and his friends. But instead of explaining His ways, He proclaims His almighty power and puts to shame their bumbling attempts to explain suffering. On hearing the voice of God, Job humbles himself and repents of his questioning of God:

> *I have heard of You by the hearing of the ear,*
> *But now my eye sees You.*
> *Therefore I abhor myself,*
> *And repent in dust and ashes.*
> JOB 42:5-6

But that wasn't the end of Job's story. In the last chapter of his book we are told that "the LORD blessed the latter days of Job more than his beginning," giving him a superabundance of livestock and ten more children (Job 42:12-15). Thus Job was amply rewarded for his patience, his faith, and his complete trust in God's power.

We should not take this to mean that all who suffer disaster will have everything restored in this life. The promise is that no matter what those who love God suffer here, a time is coming when God's blessings will cause us to forget every pain we ever endured.

Famed devotional author Hannah Whitall Smith was plagued with terrible pain and unanswered questions. It seemed to her, just as it seems to you and me, that no one could possibly understand what she was experiencing. She didn't know where to turn for help until she was told of a deeply spiritual Christian woman living nearby:

> I summoned up my courage, therefore, one
> afternoon, and went to see her, and poured out my
> troubles; expecting that of course she would take a
> deep interest in me, and would be at great pains to
> do all she could to help me. . . . When I had finished
> my story, and had paused, expecting sympathy and
> consideration, she simply said, "Yes, all you say may
> be very true, but then in spite of it all, there is God."
> I waited a few minutes for something more,
> but nothing came, and my friend and teacher had

the air of having said all that was necessary. "But," I continued, "surely you did not understand how very serious and perplexing my difficulties are."

"Oh, yes, I did," replied my friend, "but then, as I tell you, there is God." And I could not induce her to make any other answer. It seemed to me most disappointing and unsatisfactory. I felt that my peculiar and really harrowing experiences could not be met by anything so simple as merely the statement, "Yes, but there is God." . . .

At last . . . I came gradually to believing, that, being my Creator and Redeemer, He must be enough; and at last a conviction burst upon me that He really was enough, and my eyes were opened to the fact of the absolute and utter all-sufficiency of God.[13]

God is enough. Do these words of guidance seem to you as they did at first to Hannah—a trite oversimplification? They could be viewed that way until, like Hannah, we think a little more deeply. The fact is, God *must* be enough, for if He isn't, where do we go for plan B? If the God of heaven and earth—who is mightier than all the world's armies, who can cause the earth to melt into the sea—is not Lord of your crisis, you're in deep trouble. And so am I.

God *is* sufficient. He is in control. He holds the destiny of the galaxies in His hands, all the while knowing the precise number of hairs on your head. Above all else, He loves you and chose to pour that love out, not in words, but in blood.

So let the winds blow. Let the earth itself open beneath us. We place our hope in God alone, who is our fortress. And He is enough:

> God is our refuge and strength,
> A very present help in trouble.
> Therefore we will not fear,
> Even though the earth be removed,
> And though the mountains be carried into the midst
>   of the sea;
> Though its waters roar and be troubled,
> Though the mountains shake with its swelling.
>
> PSALM 46:1-3

CHAPTER 6

HOPE AFTER LOSS

Yea, though I walk through the valley of the shadow of death,
I will fear no evil; for You are with me.

PSALM 23:4

In the mid 1970s, high-tech workers in Los Angeles began constructing a new generation of spaceships. The first to be launched was the space shuttle *Columbia*, the flagship of NASA's new fleet.

Columbia blasted off April 12, 1981, and orbited the earth thirty-six times. Twenty-seven missions followed, but *Columbia's* final trip was a flight to tragedy. While reentering earth's atmosphere at nine o'clock (EST) on the morning of February 1, 2003, the shuttle broke apart. A piece of insulating foam the size of a small briefcase had peeled off during launch sixteen days earlier and punctured one of the vessel's wings. The intense heat of reentry caused gases to penetrate the wing, triggering the catastrophe that killed the seven astronauts. Debris fell across large parts of Texas and Louisiana as thousands of people gazed upward in horror.

Several years later, a poignant report emerged about the destruction of *Columbia*. While the mission was in progress, NASA specialists studying the punctured wing questioned whether the damage was fatal. Wayne Hale, the space shuttle program manager, recalls these words of flight director Jon Harpold: "You know, there is nothing we can do about damage to the TPS [thermal protection system]. If it has been damaged it's probably better not to know. I think the crew would rather not know. Don't you think it would be better for them to have a happy successful flight and die unexpectedly during entry than to stay on orbit, knowing there was nothing to be done, until the air ran out?"[1]

Harpold's question was a speculative one—should the crew be told *if* it was determined that the damage meant doom. Further analysis, however, led mission control to conclude that Columbia's reentry would be safe. The crew was given a full report of NASA's conclusion, and no one on the ship or on the ground had any expectation that the damage would prove fatal.

So neither NASA nor the *Columbia* crew ever knew the situation was hopeless before their spacecraft broke apart 207,000 feet above Texas. Evidence shows that even in the final moments of the flight, the crew was still desperately trying to regain control of the ship and safely reenter the atmosphere.

But the hypothetical question raised by Jon Harpold remains a haunting one. What would you do if you knew the crew was doomed? Would you tell them, causing indescribable mental anguish but giving them time to say their good-byes, reflect on life, and perhaps make peace with God? Or would you remain silent, making their final hours a time of exhilaration and anticipation of reunion with their loved ones?[2]

In a way, the plight of *Columbia* resembles our own: we're flying through space on a spinning planet, and every person is subject to sudden death at any moment. None of us will escape. The difference is, we all know we are going to die, and we have the opportunity to prepare!

Our Attitudes toward Death

Death. Your favorite subject? It's not mine, either. I'm not trying to cloud up your day, but I want to point out that for many people, death is the ultimate fear and the ultimate confusion. When someone dies, I hear a lot of people saying, "He's in a better place," even though before the death they tried with all their might to pray him away from that place.

Woody Allen once said, "It's not that I'm afraid of dying, I just don't want to be there when it happens."[3] Apparently he has given the matter some thought, because this comment is also attributed to him: "I don't want to achieve immortality through my work. I want to achieve immortality through not dying. I don't want to live on in the hearts of my countrymen; I would rather live on in my apartment."

We treat death as the ultimate obscene word. Rather than simply saying, "He died," we plug in an endless supply of euphemisms: "Passed on." "Went to a better place." "Was called home." "Went to sleep." "Departed this life." Or if Shakespeare is your thing, "shuffled off this mortal coil." The poet John Betjeman wanted to know, "Why do people waste their breath inventing dainty names for death?"[4]

In his book *The Hour of Our Death*, historian Philippe Ariès notes that death used to be taken more casually as a part of life. Young people weren't shielded from it. Folks died at home, and the body was put on display there. People came by to weep and mourn their loss, but no one pretended a death hadn't occurred, as we often do today when we gather in little groups in the parking lot after funerals and nervously tell jokes.[5]

Because of our discomfort, we airbrush the whole experience. We pretend people aren't going to die, and we change the subject when they wish to discuss it. Then we dispatch them from this life in white, sterilized hospital corridors, cutting them off from home and the familiar. Most of us go to great lengths to avert our eyes from the reality of death.

Joseph Bayly says that death is the great leveler of the mighty and the lowly. It plays no favorites and cuts no deals:

Dairy farmer and sales executive live in death's
shadow, with Nobel Prize winner and prostitute,

mother, infant, teen, old man. The hearse stands waiting for the surgeon who transplants a heart as well as the hopeful recipient, for the funeral director as well as the corpse he manipulates. Death spares none.[6]

Right about now, you may be thinking about skipping to the next chapter, hoping it will address a more "manageable" fear. I feel your trepidation, my friend, but just hear me out. What if I promised you that we could forever change the way you look at death—perhaps move it out of the fear category entirely? Isn't it taking up too much space in your anxiety closet? It's the idea of facing the unknown that frightens people. So let's take on this subject and, with the Bible as our guide, pull death out of the terrifying darkness once and for all.

The Fact of Death

The Bible isn't afraid to speak of death: it calls it what it is. Words such as *die* and *death* occur nearly nine hundred times in the New King James Version of the Bible. The biblical terms for death are often graceful and poetic: "gathered to my people" (Genesis 49:29); "gather[ed] . . . to your fathers, . . . gathered to your grave in peace" (2 Kings 22:20). Who isn't moved by the image of "the valley of the shadow of death" (Psalm 23:4)? I consider the following to be the most beautiful verse in the Bible concerning the death of God's people:

Precious in the sight of the LORD
Is the death of His saints.

PSALM 116:15

From the time of Adam's fall, death in the Bible is presented as a part of life. The writer of Hebrews sums it up succinctly: "It is appointed for men to die once, but after this the judgment" (Hebrews 9:27). The countdown to death begins at birth. You and I are dying at this very moment. Given that fact, how is it possible that the Bible can treat the death of believers so lightly?

The answer lies in a paradox: though death begins when we are born, life begins when we are born again by the Spirit of God through faith in Christ. Many Christians have the mistaken notion that eternal life begins when they die. But that is not biblically accurate. Eternal life begins when we are born again into the Kingdom of God. Jesus Himself defines eternal life this way: "This is eternal life, that they may know You, the only true God, and Jesus Christ whom You have sent" (John 17:3).

If you know God through Jesus Christ, then you are experiencing eternal life right now even though you haven't physically died. And if you are experiencing eternal life right now, death is no more than a brief interruption to that which you are already experiencing—life that has no end.

The New Testament is filled with passages conveying this positive, transitional perspective on death:

- Jesus refers to death as being "carried by the angels to Abraham's bosom" (Luke 16:22).
- Jesus tells the repentant thief who died beside Him, "Today you will be with Me in Paradise" (Luke 23:43).
- Paul describes death as being "absent from the body and . . . present with the Lord" (2 Corinthians 5:8).
- More than a dozen times death is described as "sleep"—the temporary status of the body from which it will be awakened in resurrection at the end of the age (John 11:11; Acts 7:60; 1 Thessalonians 4:13).
- Paul says to die is gain since we'll be with Christ, and he calls death "far better" than being on earth (Philippians 1:21, 23).
- When we die, our bodies (our "earthly house, this tent") will be destroyed, but we will inherit "a building from God, a house not made with hands, eternal in the heavens" (2 Corinthians 5:1).
- Death is "the last enemy that will be destroyed" (1 Corinthians 15:26).
- Those who die are "blessed" and have the ability to "rest from their labors" (Revelation 14:13).
- Jesus describes the separation of death as merely temporary: "A little while, and you will not see Me," he says. "And again a little while, and you will see Me" (John 16:16).

The Bible, then, gives us the full truth about death. It isn't something to fear, but a journey begun at birth, culminating in our final destination: being conformed to the image of Christ for all eternity (Romans 8:29).

The Faces of Death

The word *death* means "separation." The Bible speaks of three kinds of death: physical death, which is separation of the spirit and soul from the body; spiritual death, the separation of the human spirit from God in this life; and second death, the separation from God for eternity.

James describes *physical death* in this way: "The body without the spirit is dead" (James 2:26). The death of Rachel, the wife of the Old Testament patriarch Jacob, is expressed as "her soul . . . departing" (Genesis 35:18). Solomon describes the separation this way: "The spirit will return to God who gave it" (Ecclesiastes 12:7).

While on the cross, Jesus confirmed this separation between the spiritual and the physical as He experienced it, saying, "Father, 'into Your hands I commit My spirit'" (Luke 23:46). Matthew 27:50 adds that Jesus "yielded up His spirit."

We also see the distinction between physical death and spiritual death in the account of the church's first martyr: "They stoned Stephen as he was calling on God and saying, 'Lord Jesus, receive my spirit'" (Acts 7:59). When Stephen's spirit left his body, his body fell into the state we call physical death—which isn't the cessation of one's existence, as we can see by the heavenly reception of his spirit.

In physical death, the spirit and the soul leave the body and move either into the presence of God or into isolation from God. There are no exceptions; the statistics regarding death are 100 percent—except for Christians who are alive at the moment of the Rapture (1 Thessalonians 4:16-17). As the saying goes, death is still the number one killer in the world.

Spiritual death refers to our separation from God. Because of our sin, we have fallen short of the glory of God. We are separated from Him. Even though we are alive physically, we experience a separation the Bible describes as death: "The wages of sin is death" (Romans 6:23). When sin entered the world through Adam, it spread to everyone, so that all unregenerate men and women are dead spiritually—separated from God (Romans 5:12).

The last form of death, *second death*, is the final banishment from God—the final misery of the wicked in hell following the Great White Throne Judgment (Revelation 20:11) at the end of the Millennium. John describes this second death in the book of Revelation:

> The sea gave up the dead who were in it, and Death and Hades delivered up the dead who were in them. And they were judged, each one according to his works. Then Death and Hades were cast into the lake of fire. This is the second death. And anyone not found written in the Book of Life was cast into the lake of fire.
>
> REVELATION 20:13-15

I have tried to bring understanding to this subject by using a little mathematical formula: if you have been born only once, you will have to die twice. But if you have been born twice, you will have to die only once (and you may even escape that one death if Jesus returns to the earth during your lifetime).

All of us are born once (our physical birth), but if we are not born again through the Spirit and the Word of God (John 3:3-8; 1 Peter 1:23), we will die twice: once physically, when our bodies expire, and again at God's final judgment. However, if we are born the second time through trusting in Jesus Christ as our Savior, we will die physically, but then we will never die again. This is what our Lord means when He says, "I am the resurrection and the life. He who believes in Me, though he may die, he shall live. And whoever lives and believes in Me shall never die" (John 11:25-26).

I must note here that death also brings about another kind of separation—the separation from loved ones, which we feel physically, spiritually, and emotionally. The psalmist writes,

Loved one and friend You have put far from me,
And my acquaintances into darkness.
PSALM 88:18

Some years ago, I confronted cancer and the possibility of my own death. My greatest fear was that I'd leave my wife and my children alone. I could see the fear and worry in their faces, and that grieved me. By the grace of God, that separation didn't come. But for some people, the pain of loss in this life is only a foretaste of the greater pain to come when believing and nonbelieving loved ones are separated forever.

In his book *Chasing Daylight: How My Forthcoming Death Transformed My Life*, Eugene O'Kelly describes his diagnosis of terminal brain cancer at age fifty-three. In 2002 he was the CEO of KPMG, one of the largest accounting and financial services companies in the world. He received his terminal diagnosis in 2005 and died four months later, leaving behind his wife and two daughters. Yet he had reflected very deeply on this eventuality when his first child was born, years before the diagnosis:

> On the day my daughter Gina was born, the nurse placed her in Corinne's arms. I moved closer to my wife and baby girl, awed by what lay before me. My newborn daughter was staggeringly beautiful. . . . Before I could touch her, she reached out, startling me, and grabbed my finger. She held on tightly.
>
> A look of shock darkened my face.
>
> That day and the next I walked around as if in a fog. Corinne picked up on my odd, distracted behavior. Finally, she confronted me.
>
> "What's wrong?" she demanded, "You're acting very strange."
>
> I looked away.
>
> "What is it?" she asked. "Tell me."

I couldn't hide it any longer. "The moment she grabbed my finger," I said, "it hit me that someday I'll have to say good-bye to her."[7]

The believer, however, has a radically different perspective. We grieve, of course. We miss our loved ones with every fiber of our being, and our suffering is real. But we also know that the separation is not what it seems, that life consists of more than the visible. Deep in our mourning, our souls are kindled by the eternal hope of reunion with those we have lost, after which there will be no more parting.

Non-Christians only meet to part again; Christians only part to meet again.

There's a vast chasm of difference between those two outlooks. As Paul points out, we need not "sorrow as others who have no hope" (1 Thessalonians 4:13). Dr. S. I. McMillen and Dr. David E. Stern observed the truth of this in their book *None of These Diseases*: "After sitting beside hundreds of deathbeds, we have seen this recurring pattern. People with a strong faith tend to die in peace. People without faith tend to die in terror and torment."[8]

In his book *Fear Not!: Death and the Afterlife from a Christian Perspective*, Ligon Duncan explains that believers are animated by a hope that affects positively this life as well as the one to come:

The apostle Paul says emphatically, "If in this life only we have hope in Christ, we are of all people most to be pitied" (1 Cor. 15:19). "If the dead are not raised, 'Let us eat and drink, for tomorrow we die!'" (verse 32b). . . . He is not simply trusting in Christ so that this life might be more full or more prosperous; instead, he is trusting in Christ for this life and forevermore. . . . Christian hope is a hope that not only controls our present living, but also our anticipation of what will come to be beyond this life.[9]

The Fear of Death

I heard a story about a man who goes to the doctor for his annual physical. As he leaves, the doctor promises to call with the results. A couple of days pass before the call comes. The doctor says, "Are you seated? I'm afraid I have some bad news for you."

The man turns pale and tells the doctor to continue.

"Well," the doctor says, "you've got forty-eight hours to live."

"What?" the man stammers.

"Now for the worst," the doctor says.

"How could anything be any worse than that?" the man shouts.

"Well, it's just that I've been trying to call you since yesterday."

Calls like this happen only in bad jokes. But doctors make similar calls bearing fatal news every day. While life has no two-minute warning, time does run out. Don't we want to have our lives, our homes, and our eternal souls in order when that moment comes?

We say we want to be ready, but the problem is, death is high on our fear list. We'd rather not talk about it. So in this section of the chapter, I want to present biblical reasons that death should not be feared. If you are a Christian who remains apprehensive about death, even a little bit, I want this section to encourage you to replace your fear with biblical hope and assurance. I pray that the biblical truths presented here will move you toward faith in Christ so that His life, not your death, brings you to joyful anticipation of the future.

There are only two ways to face the future: with fear or with faith. Those who live by faith in the Son of God (Galatians 2:20) will find all their fears—especially the fear of death—consumed by the security of His person and the certainty of His promises.

The Prince of Death Has Been Defeated

The author of the book of Hebrews declares that Jesus conquered death by death, freeing us from the fear of death:

> Inasmuch then as the children have partaken of flesh
> and blood, He Himself likewise shared in the same, that
> through death He might destroy him who had the power
> of death, that is, the devil, and release those who through
> fear of death were all their lifetime subject to bondage.
> HEBREWS 2:14-15

From the Garden of Eden until Jesus' sacrificial death, the devil used death to gain the upper hand and enjoy the last laugh. Satan stirred in people the desire to violate God's laws and then watched them reap death—the reward of their sin. Paul writes that "the sting of death is sin, and the strength of sin is the law" (1 Corinthians 15:56). It was quite a system. We failed to be obedient, and we died for it—every time.

In His death and resurrection, the Son of God played the devil's own trump card. Just as David took the sword of Goliath and cut off his head with it, Jesus took the weapon of Satan and defeated him with it. The Cross must have seemed like the ultimate victory for Satan, but it was precisely the opposite. When Christ by His own death paid the penalty for sin, He took the sting out of the devil's condemnation.

When Jesus stepped from the open tomb on Resurrection Sunday, Satan's defeat was certain. His weapon of death had been destroyed. He is still alive and active, but his failure is a foregone conclusion. He must settle for winning the smaller battles, because the war he started has been lost forever.

Satan's last hope is to convince you to live as if the victory of Christ never happened. He would love for you to be enslaved to the fear of death. The first-century Jewish philosopher Philo wrote that "nothing is so calculated to enslave the mind as fearing death."[10] The author of Hebrews, undoubtedly a learned Jewish Christian, may have been aware of Philo's words, for he expresses the same sentiment, saying those who fear death "were all their lifetime subject to bondage" (Hebrews 2:15). If you do fear death, your fright is based on a lie. It is God's truth that will set you free (John 8:32).

Steve and Ann Campbell of Hampton, Tennessee, were sitting in their breakfast room one day, reading and relaxing. Their little dog, Gigi, a Maltipoo (Maltese and poodle mix), was asleep on the bench in the bay window. Suddenly a jolt rocked the room and toppled Gigi from the bench. Nothing was hurt but the little dog's pride. The couple wondered what had caused all the commotion. They couldn't find any clues until they spotted a large hawk outside lying beneath the bay window. The bird had swooped down, talons out, to get Gigi with no regard for the protective pane of glass. A few minutes later, the hawk shook off its stupor and vanished into the sky, minus its canine snack.

The devil wants to get his talons into us. The power of the Resurrection, however, provides a pane of protection that cannot be broken. Satan may knock himself out trying, but he can't claim us. Because Christ died, we have lives that are *forgiven*; because Christ rose, we have lives that are *forever*.

The Power of Death Has Been Destroyed

The prophet Isaiah, in an outburst of hope, predicts a day when the Lord will destroy death and restore His people:

> *He will swallow up death forever,*
> *And the Lord GOD will wipe away tears from all faces;*
> *The rebuke of His people*

He will take away from all the earth;
For the LORD has spoken.

ISAIAH 25:8

Hosea, a contemporary of Isaiah, also foretells Christ's victory over death:

I will ransom them from the power of the grave;
I will redeem them from death.
O Death, I will be your plagues!
O Grave, I will be your destruction!

HOSEA 13:14

These two prophecies are the first in the Bible to declare that death itself would die. The New Testament leaves no doubt as to the meaning of these words:

When this corruptible has put on incorruption, and this
mortal has put on immortality, then shall be brought to pass
the saying that is written: "Death is swallowed up in victory."

"O Death, where is your sting?
O Hades, where is your victory?"

The sting of death is sin, and the strength of sin is the
law. But thanks be to God, who gives us the victory
through our Lord Jesus Christ.

1 CORINTHIANS 15:54-57

In the book of Revelation, the apostle John describes what life will be like in heaven when these prophecies are fulfilled: "God will wipe away every tear from their eyes; there shall be no more death, nor sorrow, nor crying. There shall be no more pain, for the former things have passed away" (Revelation 21:4).

The apostle Paul reminds Timothy that through His resurrection, Christ has "abolished death and brought life and immortality to light through the gospel" (2 Timothy 1:10).

And in one of the most poignant passages in the New Testament on the inviolability of God's love for His children, Paul includes death in the list of realities that will never separate us from that love:

> I am persuaded that neither death nor life, nor angels nor principalities nor powers, nor things present nor things to come, nor height nor depth, nor any other created thing, shall be able to separate us from the love of God which is in Christ Jesus our Lord.
>
> ROMANS 8:38-39

Jesse Irvin Overholtzer, the founder of Child Evangelism Fellowship (CEF), was growing old. He knew he had few remaining years in this life. He and his wife, Ruth, invited a young nurse from India to stay with them while she attended classes at the nearby CEF Institute. When Overholtzer suffered a seizure, she was up with him throughout the night.

Yet at dawn she took off for classes as if she'd gotten a full night's sleep.

"Isn't it wonderful to be young and full of life?" Ruth said to her husband.

"Yes," Overholtzer answered, "but it is more wonderful to be old and ready to go to heaven!"[11]

The Process of Death Has Been Described

An eleven-year-old wrote to Pope John Paul with this question: "What is it like when you die? Nobody will tell me. I just want to know, but I don't want to do it."[12] Jesus tells a story in Luke 16:19-31 that offers a penetrating view of what happens after death. In fact, this story tells us more about life after death than we might expect.

His parable concerns two men—one rich and one poor. The pauper's name is Lazarus (though not the same man Jesus raised from the dead). We don't know the rich man's name, but we know his lifestyle. He wears the finest clothing and eats the finest cuisine. He has the best of everything, and he lets everyone know about it—even Lazarus, the beggar at his gates, who hopes to be thrown a few crumbs from the bountiful table. Lazarus is not only hungry but also very ill, covered with sores that the town dogs lick. His is a miserable existence.

Lazarus, however, possesses one thing that no one can take away: his love for God. The rich man possesses one thing he cannot keep: his life. Both men die. On the other side of the gate that separates this life from eternity, the beggar Lazarus is carried by heavenly angels to the bosom of Abraham. Now he is kissed by angels rather than licked by dogs.

So it will be for you and me. We won't simply be "beamed up" to heaven. We will be carried there by angels. This passage provides one of the euphemisms we employ for death: "The angels took him." It may sound like a cliché from a Victorian greeting card, but it is biblical truth as applied to believers in Christ. On the day when you wait for the curtains to be drawn on this life, God's messengers stand ready to bear you away on life's ultimate journey. The great hymn writer Isaac Watts expressed it in fine poetry:

> *Lord, when I leave this mortal ground,*
> *And thou shalt bid me rise and come,*
> *Send a beloved angel down,*
> *Safe to conduct my spirit home.*[13]

In his children's book *Somewhere Angels*, Larry Libby suggests that God sends angels so we won't have to make that journey alone. Great voyages need great companions, and God says, "When it's your time to come, I'll send someone to bring you. You won't need to fear; you won't need to find your own way. And the person I will send knows the way very well."[14] At the moment when you first set eyes on your forever home, an angel will be there to share your joy. As you realize you've now been made perfect, with every ailment gone, an angel will be there to laugh with you, to hear your shouts of triumph.

On that journey, Christians will experience none of the travel worries we face now—no getting lost, no missing the bus, no waiting for the next plane. God has an angel assigned to bring you home. In the face of such assurance, how can we fear?

The Picture of Death Has Been Developed

On December 7, 1941, Rev. Peter Marshall was speaking to the cadets at Annapolis. A "day of infamy" was unfolding at Pearl Harbor, which now lay in the flames of an enemy attack. The room was filled with young men who would soon sacrifice their lives for their country. He told them the story of a dying child—a little boy with a disease who asked his mother, "What is it like to die? Does it hurt?" The mother thought for a minute, then said, "Do you remember when you were smaller, and you played very hard and fell asleep on your mommy's bed? You awoke to find yourself somehow in your own bed. Your daddy had come along, with his big, strong arms and lifted you, undressed you, put you into your pajamas as you slept. Honey, that's what death is like. It's waking up in your own room."[15]

Like this little boy, most of us are curious about the process of death. Perhaps no single verse of Scripture gives us a more comforting picture of it than the widely quoted Psalm 23:4:

Yea, though I walk through the valley of the shadow of death,
I will fear no evil;
For You are with me;
Your rod and Your staff, they comfort me.

The sheer beauty of the passage never fails to move us, of course. But the power of this truth hits us at a deep level in times of suffering. When we face death—our own or the death of a loved one—this verse should be held close to our hearts. Its poetic phrases teach us several things.

DEATH IS A JOURNEY, NOT A DESTINATION

I walk through the valley. . . .
PSALM 23:4

Pastor and author Leith Anderson tells of a woman who buried her husband after he lost a battle with cancer. A short time later, she found that the same disease had come for her. She could only await her reunion with the husband she had loved and lost.

When she knew she had only a few days left, the woman invited Anderson and his wife to her home. They sat with deep emotion, holding her hands as she spoke casually of the reality of death and anticipating her joy in the presence of God. She talked about her children and wanted to know all about the Andersons' kids. You'd have thought she was preparing for a cruise instead of a departure from this life.

A constant stream of friends came to comfort her, but it was the other way around. They left deeply blessed. And those who couldn't visit heard encouragement from her on the phone. Through it all, she never thought of herself. Everything she did illustrated her concern and love for others. Her hope for the afterlife enabled her to use death as an opportunity to reach out and bless as many people as possible.[16]

Most of us speak of hope for the afterlife. But the way we approach death shows what we really believe. Those committed to a biblical perspective have no reason to treat death as their greatest enemy. They see it as another journey that calls for preparation. They say their good-byes, they get their affairs in order, and they prepare their spirits for the joy of a new existence.

As we know, many people today believe this life is all there is—that physical death and spiritual death are one and the same and that their entire existence will come to an end. For people who believe this way, it's perfectly reasonable to fear death. They think it's the final curtain. Believing this life to be all there is, they clutch it tightly. To these people, life must be a source of deep frustration and even despair because it has so many limitations, so much disappointment. You come into the world, you're young and strong, then you reach the top of the hill and begin a long, sad descent—and at the bottom lurks nothing but darkness.

Christians, however, live in a brighter now because everything in life has a reason. The ups and downs point to an eternity that will fulfill all our hopes and repay all our frustrations. Poor Lazarus had reason for hope. He knew what other hurting believers know—that this world was never their home anyway. They are citizens of heaven, ambassadors of a bright reality.

We must remember that for believers and nonbelievers

alike, death is not the end. We are all eternal creatures. The distinction is whether one's eternity will be brighter than a billion suns or darker than the imagination can conceive.

In the "Shepherd Psalm," David sees death not as a destination but as a journey through a dark country—a journey we make with God's hand in ours. My friend Pastor Rob Morgan describes how this journey reveals the transitory nature of death:

> Psalm 23:4 does not speak of a cave or a dead-end trail. It's a valley, which means it has an opening on both ends. . . . The emphasis is on *through*, which indicates a temporary state, a transition, a brighter path ahead, a hopeful future. For Christians, problems are always temporary and blessings always eternal (as opposed to non-Christians, whose blessings are temporal and whose problems are eternal). Valleys don't go on forever, and the road ahead is always bright for the child of God, as bright as His promises. There are no cul-de-sacs on His maps, no blind alleys in His will, no dead ends in His guidance.[17]

Paul speaks of being "absent from the body and . . . present with the Lord," indicating that the two conditions are one and the same (2 Corinthians 5:8). As James M. Campbell observed, death is an exit gate and heaven is an entrance. But the two are arranged so closely that one opens as the other shuts. When one person says that a dying person is "lying at the gates of death," another could say that, no, he is "lying at the gate of heaven." And both would have it right.[18]

DEATH IS A SHADOW, NOT A REALITY

The valley of the shadow of death . . .
PSALM 23:4

When I was a young boy, my father was the pastor of a church in Toledo, Ohio. During his eleven-year pastorate there, the church relocated to a property that had once been a luxurious mansion. The mansion was restored and an auditorium was built on one end of it, and that became our new church.

Behind this mansion was a huge ten-car garage. The parsonage was on the second floor of the garage in what had formerly been the servants' quarters. One of my nightly chores was to carry out the trash to containers located outside the cavernous garage. When I waited until after dark to do my chores, I had to carry the trash through the eerie, dimly lit garage. At night it was a foreboding place, filled with shadows that seemed to hide unthinkable horrors. In my terror, I ran through those shadows, possibly setting new speed records for trash-and-carry.

During daylight hours I could clearly see that I was in no danger—no monsters lurked in that garage. But darkness does something to a place, doesn't it? It distorts. It becomes a canvas for the imagination. The good news is that shadows are only the deflection of light. They can frighten, but they can do no harm.

As Dr. Donald Grey Barnhouse was driving home from the funeral of his first wife, he and his children were overcome with grief. As he sought some word of comfort for his kids, a huge moving van passed them, and its shadow swept over the car. Dr. Barnhouse said, "Children, would you rather be run over by a truck or by its shadow?"

"The shadow, of course," one of the children said. "It's harmless."

"Two thousand years ago," the father said, "the truck ran over the Lord Jesus . . . in order that only its shadow might run over us."[19]

For the Christian, death is but a shadow. No longer is it the true substance of our fear; it's just a momentary obscuring of the light. Jesus' promise to every believer is this: "Because I live, you will live also" (John 14:19). He also says, "I am the resurrection and the life. He who believes in Me, though he may die, he shall live. And whoever lives and believes in Me shall never die" (John 11:25-26).

DEATH IS LONELY, BUT YOU ARE NEVER ALONE

You are with me. . . .

PSALM 23:4

Something strange but subtle happens in Psalm 23:4. You may not have noticed, but an editor would. The narrative mode changes: *He* becomes *You*. In the first three verses, we've seen the Lord referred to in the third person: "*He* makes me to lie down; *He* restores; *He* leads me . . . for *His* name's sake."

Very abruptly, however, third person becomes second person, and David says, "*You* are with me." He stops talking *about* the Shepherd and begins talking *to* Him. It's as if he has been talking about God, and then in the midst of the shadows he realizes that God is right there: "I will fear no evil; for *You* are with me." An essay becomes an intimate conversation.

It all makes beautiful sense if you've ever walked through that valley. You think about God, and suddenly you find yourself caught up in a conversation with Him. His presence suddenly changes your whole line of thought. Over the years, I've spoken to many people who were traveling their darkest roads, and they've often told me that they were never more aware of the presence of the Shepherd than when they were walking in that shadow.

Corrie ten Boom once ran into an old friend who was only going to be in town for the day. So they dispensed with small talk and had a substantial conversation together. Corrie asked him, "Are you afraid to die?"

Yes, he was, he admitted. Corrie was surprised, knowing that her friend had a deep faith in God. She asked, "Why are you afraid? You've been a believer for as long as I've known you. Surely you know Jesus won't leave you alone for one moment."

He explained that he was afraid because death was the unknown for him; he didn't know what to expect. So they began talking about Jesus and how death was also unknown to Him when He went to the Cross. He had never died before. Surely He, too, had to confront fear. But now Jesus knows all about death. He has been there. He has conquered it. And He promises never to leave or forsake us. He says He will be with us always, and the journey through death is no exception.

The old man smiled, at peace, and thanked God for the conversation.[20]

I've counseled with many people as they sat in death's waiting room, and experience has proved to me that God makes His presence known as they walk through the valley. He reaches for their hands. He whispers words of comfort and promise. And it's not limited just to the dying people themselves; it's also for those who grieve for them. They, too, walk through the valley, and God reaches to them as well.

The Bible is filled with comforting promises such as these:

God is our refuge and strength,
A very present help in trouble.
Therefore we will not fear.
PSALM 46:1-2

He Himself has said, "I will never leave you nor
forsake you."
HEBREWS 13:5

Indeed, the darkness shall not hide from You,
But the night shines as the day;
The darkness and the light are both alike to You.
PSALM 139:12

We never have to walk that road alone. The Shepherd appears at our shoulder, and as we reach the gate, angels are there to attend us and usher us into the wonderful surprises that await us.

This life seems like the "real" one, but it is only a preface, and we have yet to see the first chapter. As Hungarian composer Franz Liszt expressed in the introduction to his symphonic poem *Les Preludes*, "What else is our life but a series of preludes to that unknown Hymn, the first and solemn note of which is intoned by Death?"[21] We think the story ends with death, but the truth is, death is only the beginning. The Bible grounds our hope, assuring us that what follows is too wonderful for us to understand now.

In the seven books of C. S. Lewis's Chronicles of Narnia series, four children explore another world, ruled by Aslan the Lion. In the first six books, Aslan sends them back to their home in England after each adventure. As the final book draws to its close, the children find themselves in a brilliantly enhanced Narnia, and they don't want to leave. Their own world seems pale by comparison. But Aslan has a surprise. He reveals that the railway accident that brought them to Narnia this time was a real one, and they have, in earthly terms, died and left their everyday world for the last time. "The term is over," Aslan says. "The holidays have begun. The dream is ended. This is the morning."

The great Lion then begins to transform into something that is—like the adventures facing the children—too wonderful to write about. Their lives on earth and in the old

Narnia were only "the cover and the title page," and now they are truly beginning the first chapter of the real story. It is a story that "no one on earth has read: which goes on forever: in which every chapter is better than the one before."[22]

Born in 1800, a century before Lewis, John Todd also saw the significance and hope of death. Todd was a Vermont boy who at the age of six lost both parents. He lost his siblings, too, when they were divided among relatives. John was taken in by a kindly aunt. He lived with her for fifteen years until he left to study for the ministry. The years passed, and he became an effective pastor. One day he received a letter from the aunt who raised him. She was dying, and she had the same questions we all ask: "What awaits me in death? Is this the end?" John could feel her anxiety in every line she wrote.

John loved his aunt, and he sat down to answer her letter. He began with the story of a little boy of six who waited for the arrival of the woman who would become a mother to him:

> I can still recall my disappointment when instead
> of coming for me yourself, you sent your servant,
> Caesar, to fetch me.
>   I remember my tears and my anxiety as, perched
> high on your horse and clinging tight to Caesar,
> I rode off to my new home. Night fell before we
> finished the journey, and I became lonely and afraid.
>   "Do you think she'll go to bed before I get there?"
> I asked Caesar anxiously.

"Oh no," he said reassuringly. "She'll sure stay up for you. When we get out of these here woods, you'll see her candle shining in the window."

Presently we did ride out in the clearing, and there, sure enough, was your candle. I remember you were waiting at the door, that you put your arms close about me—a tired and bewildered little boy. You had a big fire burning on the hearth, a hot supper waiting on the stove. After supper you took me to my new room, heard my prayers, and then sat beside me until I fell asleep.

Someday soon God will send for you, to take you to a new home. Don't fear the summons, the strange journey, or the dark messenger of death. God can be trusted to do as much for you as you were kind enough to do for me so many years ago. At the end of the road you will find love and a welcome awaiting, and you will be safe in God's care.[23]

John Todd painted for his aunt a picture of new life as beautiful as any person could hope for. But I can assure you that it is only a dim shadow compared to the magnificent beauty and joy awaiting us when we finally close this gate and open the new one into God's presence.

CHAPTER 7

YOUR ULTIMATE HOPE

The LORD takes pleasure in those who fear Him.

PSALM 147:11

In C. S. Lewis's Narnia book *The Silver Chair*, the schoolgirl Jill finds herself alone and desperately thirsty in an unknown wood. She knows nothing of Aslan, the Christ figure in these stories, but when she comes upon a stream, she sees the great Lion between her and the water. Though her thirst is overpowering, Jill freezes in her tracks, too petrified with terror to either advance or run.

"If you are thirsty, you may drink," the Lion says.

The terrified Jill, afraid she will be eaten, doesn't move. She says, "Will you promise not to—do anything to me, if I do come?"

"I make no promise," the Lion answers.

"I daren't come and drink," Jill replies.

"Then you will die of thirst," the Lion tells her.

Jill says she will go find another stream, but the Lion responds, "There is no other stream."[1]

Throughout the Bible God's people are admonished to fear God. Is this fear to be equated with Jill's—that of a child quivering in unmitigated terror at an all-powerful being who forces hard choices and may do anything to anyone at any time?

The same God who invites us to come boldly into His presence (Hebrews 4:16; 10:19) also expects us to "serve God acceptably with reverence and *godly fear*. For our God is a consuming fire" (Hebrews 12:28-29; emphasis added).

As one who lives in Southern California and has seen consuming wildfires up close and personal, I can say that fear is an apt description of the emotion they produce. Do they also produce a sense of awe? Yes—one cannot help but be awed by flames shooting hundreds of feet in the air and consuming everything in their paths. But is it awe that causes my neighbors and me to flee for safety when these fires are on the loose? No, it is fear of dying in their presence—not because the fire has any intent of harming us, but because fire has an innate nature that can harm us if we don't respect it. So when the author of Hebrews says "our God is a consuming fire," I am not surprised to read that I should serve Him with "godly fear." Yes, God inspires overwhelming awe. But just as fire acts according to its nature, so does God. He operates according to His providential intent for His world, and we had best align ourselves with that intent to keep from getting burned.

Two Ways to Fear God

Biblical references to the fear of God fall into two distinct categories. The first is awesome dread, and the second is astonished devotion. Let's explore the meaning of these two terms.

Awesome Dread

The term *awesome dread* seems to indicate something to avoid rather than embrace. And I realize that I have been guilty of avoiding the topic myself at times because it's so easy to stress the love of God and how Jesus is a friend of sinners. But that is only one side of the equation. Unless we balance our perspective, we end up with the idea that "there's no need to be afraid of our good buddy God."[2]

So when we go to the Bible to adjust that perspective, do we discover that *fear* is just a synonym for *awe* and *reverence*? As a matter of fact, no. In Genesis, where the word *fear* is first used in the Bible, we read about God walking in the Garden just after Adam and Eve had eaten the forbidden fruit. Apparently God made a practice of enjoying fellowship with them "in the garden in the cool of the day" (Genesis 3:8). But after Adam and Eve sinned and God drew near, Adam hid himself from God's presence. He explains, "I heard Your voice in the garden, and I was afraid because I was naked; and I hid myself" (Genesis 3:10).

I assure you that what Adam felt at that moment was much more than awe and reverence for his Creator. He was stone-cold afraid—exactly as he should have been. God had warned him that if he ate of the forbidden tree, he would die (Genesis 3:3).

We don't fear what we don't know. That's why little ones touch hot stoves once. People who are without God are without fear of Him, so they don't hesitate to act in immoral ways. In Romans 3, Paul the apostle gives us a long list of complaints about ungodly people, and in verse 18 he concludes it by quoting Psalm 36:1: "There is no fear of God before [their] eyes."

But those who know God fear Him. People in Scripture such as Abraham, Moses, Joshua, Gideon, Isaiah, Ezekiel, and Saul found this fear so overwhelming that they could not stand on their feet in His presence.

Many Christians today seem to think the Incarnation eliminated the need for any fear of God. In Jesus, God came to earth in the form of a man, giving us an accessible God, one we could love and relate to as a friend. Those who adopt this mindset as the whole truth often describe Jesus as a gentle, compassionate, loving person. He was (and is) all that, but this is not the entire picture. Forgotten is the fearsome Jesus who took a whip and single-handedly drove from the Temple a mass of thieving merchants. You can be sure that those around Him felt fear.

It is in the book of Revelation that we witness some of the most terrifying depictions of our Lord. For example, when John saw the risen Christ, he fell at His feet as dead (Revelation 1:17). This was not a voluntary act of worship but an instinctive reaction of fear.

The apostle Peter gives us what is perhaps the primary reason for our awe and dread of God. After a night of unsuccessful fishing, Peter was discouraged. Then Jesus performed a miracle that suddenly overloaded Peter's nets. "When Simon Peter saw it, he fell down at Jesus' knees, saying, 'Depart from me, for I am a sinful man, O Lord!'" (Luke 5:8). Awe and dread are natural responses of the imperfect to the perfect, of the marred to the beautiful, of the contaminated to the pure, of the powerless to the powerful.

Astonished Devotion

If awe and dread are appropriate responses to God, how do we reconcile that with Paul's confident statement in Romans 8:1? "There is therefore now no condemnation to those who are in Christ Jesus." As believers in Christ, we know we can live with absolutely no fear of the wrath of God. That's an assurance engraved in eternity.

This brings up an important question. If Christ has removed the need for fear of God's wrath, do we really need to fear God at all? Paul answers by telling us that fear still has its place. He instructs his friends in Philippi to "work out your own salvation with fear and trembling" (Philippians 2:12). Peter also affirms the role of fear when he admonishes us,

"Conduct yourselves throughout the time of your stay here in fear" (1 Peter 1:17). Why should we continue to fear God if His grace removes the consequences of His wrath?

We find the explanation in the Bible's second conception of fear. For active followers of Jesus Christ, this understanding is the most meaningful for everyday living. We fear God by honoring, reverencing, and cherishing Him. His greatness and majesty reduce us to an overpowering sense of awe that is not focused only on His wrath and judgment but also on His transcendent glory, which is like nothing else we can confront in this world. It leaves us all but speechless.

Though God had every right to judge the human race, in astounding mercy He sent His own Son to stand in judgment for us. So to fear only God's power with trembling and dread without fearing (or respecting) His astonishing love is an incomplete response that diminishes our experience and enjoyment of Him.

When we truly fear God, our fear of other things and other people begins to wane. Big fears make little fears go away. We can spend our days worrying about a host of daily challenges, but let the word *cancer* be mentioned in the same sentence with our name, and all our daily anxieties disappear into the cloud of a bigger fear. God, of course, is not a malevolent force like cancer. This means that when our smaller fears are absorbed by fear of Him, our lives gain security rather than become debilitated by the terror of an uncertain future.

God is the biggest fear of all. In fact, God is referred to

as "the Fear" twice in Genesis 31: "Unless the God of my father, the God of Abraham and the Fear of Isaac, had been with me . . . And Jacob swore by the Fear of his father Isaac" (verses 42, 53). "The Fear" is a figure of speech here in which the emotion is personified as the person Himself—in this case, God.

It is when other fears take precedence over God that we get into trouble. This is what happened to the Israelites who lived during the time of Isaiah. Listen to God's words to them:

> *Of whom have you been afraid, or feared,*
> *That you have lied*
> *And not remembered Me,*
> *Nor taken it to your heart?*
> *Is it not because I have held My peace from of old*
> *That you do not fear Me?*
> ISAIAH 57:11

In losing their fear of God, the nation of Judah had become unduly afraid of false pagan gods. They no longer felt "astonished devotion" because they had lost the wonder of who God is.

Ravi Zacharias said, "The older you get, the more it takes to fill your heart with wonder, and only God is big enough to do that."[3] No matter how old we are, we all need astonished devotion, which is the exhilarating element we find in the fear of God.

Hope for Those Who Fear God

When we consider both dimensions of the fear of God—awesome dread and astonished devotion—we discover that the Bible promises abundant benefits for those who hold these fears. The following list of seven promises summarizes why we can fear God—and put our hope in Him. I present them mostly without comment, because I believe they will minister to your heart in their raw beauty and blessing.

The Promise of Provision

Oh, fear the LORD, you His saints!
There is no want to those who fear Him.
The young lions lack and suffer hunger;
But those who seek the LORD shall not lack
    any good thing.

PSALM 34:9-10

The Promise of Protection

Behold, the eye of the LORD is on those who fear Him,
On those who hope in His mercy,
To deliver their soul from death,
And to keep them alive in famine.

PSALM 33:18-19

The Promise of Purity

As far as the east is from the west,
So far has He removed our transgressions from us.

As a father pities his children,
So the LORD pities those who fear Him.
PSALM 103:12-13

Having these promises, beloved, let us cleanse
ourselves from all filthiness of the flesh and spirit,
perfecting holiness in the fear of God.
2 CORINTHIANS 7:1

The Promise of Prosperity

Blessed is every one who fears the LORD,
Who walks in His ways.
When you eat the labor of your hands,
You shall be happy, and it shall be well with you.
PSALM 128:1-2

The Promise of Prolonged Days

The fear of the LORD prolongs days,
But the years of the wicked will be shortened.
PROVERBS 10:27

The Promise of Privilege

Those who feared the LORD spoke to one another,
And the LORD listened and heard them;
So a book of remembrance was written before Him
For those who fear the LORD
And who meditate on His name.
MALACHI 3:16

The Promise of Perpetuity

*Oh, that they had such a heart in them that they
would fear Me and always keep all My commandments,
that it might be well with them and with their children
forever!*

DEUTERONOMY 5:29

*The mercy of the LORD is from everlasting to everlasting
On those who fear Him,
And His righteousness to children's children.*

PSALM 103:17

These are only a sampling of the outpouring of promises the Bible gives to those who fear the Lord.

It's true that there is a consequence for not fearing God, but it's not as if God exacts a pound of flesh for our failure. Instead, we face the consequence of missing the blessings described above. It's more like the consequence of a child missing out on Christmas morning. Who would want to forgo the spiritual treasures of fearing God?

Yet He leaves the choice to us.

The Conclusion of the Whole Matter

Solomon spent his life questing for meaning and significance, and he concludes that it was wrapped up—yes—in "fearing God."

Let us hear the conclusion of the whole matter:
Fear God and keep His commandments,
For this is man's all.
ECCLESIASTES 12:13

Did you realize the Bible has so much to say about the fear of God? Would it surprise you to know that this fear has played a large role throughout church history? Times of spectacular spiritual revival have always been sparked by a renewal of the fear of God. The best example is the preaching of Jonathan Edwards during the First Great Awakening. During that era, Edwards, George Whitefield, and others preached on God's judgment, which brought a sense of terror over the audiences. It's hard for us to imagine today how Edwards's famous sermon "Sinners in the Hands of an Angry God" brought on moaning and weeping and prompted listeners to grip tightly to pews and posts to keep themselves from tumbling to the floor.

Reverend Joseph H. Weber, a Methodist evangelist who witnessed a revival in the town of Algona, Iowa, wrote, "It seems as if many more sinners are moved by fear than love."[4] Scottish evangelist Duncan Campbell said, "It is an entire town gripped by the fear of God, causing an awareness of God coming over the whole community."[5] During the Irish revival of 1857, a thirty-four-year-old man fell to his knees in the street, crying out in deep agony. People came rushing to his aid, asking who had attacked him. But he would only cry out, "Unclean! Unclean! God be merciful to me, a sinner!"[6]

Wesley L. Duewel, in his book *Revival Fire*, said that the fear of God was so sudden and so powerful in these times of revival that whole communities came to Christ. Hardened men began weeping. Miracles occurred. Addicts were made clean, homes were restored, and local crime was all but wiped out. The fear of God changed everything. Duewel goes on to record this quote: "They were first affected with awe and fear—then they were bathed in tears—then filled with love unspeakable."[7]

It's a sad fact that something so well established in the history books is so difficult for us to visualize today. As a culture, we have no fear of God; so, as Dostoyevsky said, "All things are permissible." We see no miracles. We are flooded with addictions; broken homes; and rampant, uncontrollable crime. Yet some Christians say we need less "fear of God" in our teaching, though they're all for "love of God" talk. But as we have seen, the road to love leads right through the fear of God.

I will close with a passage from pastor and author John Piper, who imagines a scenario from nature to illustrate what it means to fear God's power and put our hope in His protection:

Suppose you were exploring an unknown glacier in the north of Greenland in the dead of winter. Just as you reach a sheer cliff with a spectacular view of miles and miles of jagged ice and mountains of snow, a terrible storm breaks in. The wind is so strong that the fear rises in your heart that it might blow you over the cliff. But in the midst of the storm you discover a cleft in the ice where you can hide. Here you feel secure. But, even though secure, the awesome might of the storm rages on, and you watch it with a kind of trembling pleasure as it surges out across the distant glaciers.

At first there was the fear that this terrible storm and awesome terrain might claim your life. But then you found a refuge and gained the hope that you would be safe. But not everything in the feeling called fear vanished from your heart. Only the life-threatening part. There remained the trembling, the awe, the wonder, the feeling that you would never want to tangle with such a storm or be the adversary of such a power.

And so it is with God. . . . The fear of God is what is left of the storm when you have a safe place to watch right in the middle of it. . . . Hope turns fear into a trembling and peaceful wonder; and fear takes everything trivial out of hope and makes it earnest and profound. The terrors of God make the pleasures of his people intense. The fireside fellowship is all the sweeter when the storm is howling outside the cottage.[8]

I am thankful that my God is a fearsome God. My love for Him is all the deeper for the fear that His love has answered. The storm rages all around, but my hope is in Him.

Acknowledgments

Writing this book was like writing ten books. Every chapter was a project of its own. It has taken everything I had to give, and without the support of my wife, Donna, my "everything" would not have been enough. My older son, David Michael, has become a strong partner in the publishing arm of our ministry, and I wish to thank him for his help. Paul Joiner and his creative team continue to be the best in the business. Thank you for the countless hours you spent dreaming and planning for the release of this book. Diane Sutherland stands at the door of my life and graciously protects the resources of my time and energy. She and Barbara Boucher deserve more credit than they ever get for dealing with the increasing demands that are placed upon our offices.

Along with the personal side of publishing, there is also a more public side. I am very grateful for Sealy Yates, my agent and confidant. I am delighted to be working with Ron Beers and Tyndale House Publishers. I am indebted to William Kruidenier, Rob Morgan, Rob Suggs, and Tom Williams, who have invested their gifts in this project.

Finally, thank you to Beau Sager, who worked so many hours checking and chasing down quotes, working with editors, and making many valuable suggestions about the substance and sequencing of the material.

To do what we do each year would be beyond impossible without you, and I thank you, each one!

Notes

INTRODUCTION

1. Linda Lyons, "What Frightens America's Youth?" Gallup.com, March 29, 2005, www.gallup.com/poll/15439/What-Frightens-Americas-Youth.aspx.

CHAPTER 1: HOPE IN THE MIDST OF THE STORM

1. Sebastian Junger, *The Perfect Storm: A True Story of Men against the Sea* (New York: W. W. Norton & Company, 2009), 106.
2. Craig Brian Larson and *Leadership Journal, 750 Engaging Illustrations for Preachers, Teachers, and Writers* (Grand Rapids, MI: Baker Books, 2007), 493.
3. James Paton, John Gibson Paton, *Missionary to the New Hebrides: An Autobiography*, volume 2 (London: Butler & Tanner, 1889), 192.
4. Paton, 325.
5. Joni Eareckson Tada, *Hope . . . the Best of Things* (Wheaton, IL: Crossway Books, 2008), 16.
6. C. S. Lewis, *The Problem of Pain* (New York: Macmillan Publishing Company, Inc., 1973), 84.
7. Ruth A. Tucker, *From Jerusalem to Irian Jaya* (Grand Rapids, MI: Zondervan, 1983, 2004), 137.
8. Charles Haddon Spurgeon, "Fearing and Trusting—Trusting and Not Fearing," *Sermons on the Psalms* (London: Marshall, Morgan & Scott, 1963).

CHAPTER 2: HOPE AFTER FAILURE

1. Robert A. Caro, *The Passage of Power*, vol. 4 of *The Years of Lyndon Johnson* (New York: Alfred A. Knopf, 2012), 16.
2. Caro, 21.

3. From the Special Features segment of *The Fugitive*, © 1993 Warner Bros. Pictures.

4. J. Oswald Sanders, *Robust in Faith* (Chicago: Moody Press, 1965), 72.

5. William Sykes, *The Eternal Vision: The Ultimate Collection of Spiritual Quotations* (Peabody, MA: Hendrickson Publishers, 2003), 70.

6. Paul Laurence Dunbar, "Right's Security" in *Lyrics of Lowly Life* (New York: Dodd, Mead and Company, 1898), 179.

7. J. I. Packer, *Knowing God* (Downers Grove, IL: InterVarsity Press, 1973), 23.

CHAPTER 3: HOPE DURING A FINANCIAL COLLAPSE

1. Henry David Thoreau, *Walden* (New York: Barnes and Noble Books, 2004), 74.

2. John Wesley, *Selections from the Writings of the Rev. John Wesley* (New York: Methodist Book Concern, 1929), 232.

3. John Wesley, *Sermons on Several Occasions*, volume 1 (London, 1829), 566.

4. Timothy George, "Unseen Footprints," *Preaching Today* audio, no. 290.

5. Adapted from Robert J. Morgan, *On This Day* (Nashville: Thomas Nelson, 1997), March 12.

6. Leonard Griffith, *God in Man's Experience: The Activity of God in the Psalms* (Waco, TX: Word Books, 1968), 59–60.

7. Charles H. Spurgeon, "The Treasury of David: Psalm 37," Christianity.com, https://www.christianity.com/bible/commentary.php?com=spur&b=19&c=37.

8. From Leonard I. Sweet, *Strong in the Broken Places* (Akron, OH: University of Akron, 1995), 109.

9. Philip Yancey, *The Jesus I Never Knew* (Grand Rapids, MI: Zondervan, 1995), 275.

CHAPTER 4: HOPE AMID SERIOUS ILLNESS

1. David Jeremiah, *When Your World Falls Apart* (Nashville: Thomas Nelson, 2000), 38.

2. Isobel Kuhn, *In the Arena* (Singapore: OMF Books, 1960), 225–232.

3. Centers for Disease Control and Prevention, "FastStats: Leading Causes of Death," January 11, 2013, www.cdc.gov/nchs/fastats/lcod.htm.

4. Ezra Klein, "21 Graphs That Show America's Health-Care Prices Are Ludicrous," *The Washington Post*, March 26, 2013, www.washingtonpost.com/blogs/wonkblog//2013/03/26/21-graphs-that-show-americas-health-care-prices-are-ludicrous.

5. "National Health Expenditure Data: Historical," CMS.gov, www.cms.gov/Research-Statistics-Data-and-Systems/Statistics-Trends-and-Reports/NationalHealthExpendData/NationalHealthAccountsHistorical.

6. C. S. Lewis, "The Efficacy of Prayer" in *The World's Last Night and Other Essays* (New York: Harcourt, Brace & World, 1960), 9.

7. Randy Alcorn, *We Shall See God: Charles Spurgeon's Classic Devotional Thoughts on Heaven* (Carol Stream, IL: Tyndale House Books, 2011), 298.

8. Kuhn, *In the Arena*, 225–232.

9. Amy Carmichael, *Gold by Moonlight: Sensitive Lessons from a Walk with Pain* (Fort Washington, PA: CLC Publications, 2013), chapter 10.

10. Ed Dobson, *Prayers and Promises When Facing a Life-Threatening Illness* (Grand Rapids, MI: Zondervan, 2007), 56.

11. Thomas Watson, *A Divine Cordial: Romans 8:28* (La Vergne, TN: Lightning Source, Inc., 2001), 20.

12. Kuhn, *In the Arena*, 252–232.

13. Kuhn, 252–232.

14. Adapted from Robert J. Morgan, *From This Verse* (Nashville: Thomas Nelson, 1998), August 13.

15. Robert J. Morgan, *Real Stories for the Soul* (Nashville: Thomas Nelson, 2000), 1–3.

16. Morgan, 1–3.

17. Author unknown, quoted by Curtis C. Thomas, *Practical Wisdom for Pastors* (Wheaton, IL: Crossway Books, 2001), 102.

CHAPTER 5: HOPE WHEN FACING DISASTER

1. George H. Smith, *Atheism: The Case against God* (New York: Prometheus Books, 1979), 81.

2. Allan Laing, "Wave That Beggared My Belief," *The Herald* (Glasgow, Scotland), January 4, 2005.

3. C. S. Lewis, *Mere Christianity* (New York: The Macmillan Company, 1952), 31.

4. Erwin Lutzer, *Where Was God?: Answers to Tough Questions about God and Natural Disasters* (Carol Stream, IL: Tyndale House Publishers, 2006), 100.

5. Dinesh D'Souza, *What's So Great about Christianity* (Washington, DC: Regnery Publishing, 2007), 278.

6. James Montgomery Boice, *Romans Volume 2: The Reign of Grace* (Grand Rapids, MI: Baker Book House, 1992), 906.

7. Donald Grey Barnhouse, *God's Heirs: Romans 8:1-39* (Grand Rapids, MI: Wm. B. Eerdmans Publishing Co., 1959), 153.

8. Annie Johnson Flint, quoted in Mrs. Charles Cowman, *Streams in the Desert* (Grand Rapids, MI: Zondervan Publishing House, 1966), 148–149.

9. "The American Colony in Jerusalem," Library of Congress, December 1, 2008, www.loc.gov/exhibits/americancolony/amcolony-family.html.

10. Lutzer, *Where Was God*, 104.
11. Mark Mittelberg, *The Questions Christians Hope No One Will Ask* (Carol Stream, IL: Tyndale House Publishers, 2010), 137.
12. Adapted from Ray Stedman, *Let God Be God: Life-Changing Truths from the Book of Job* (Grand Rapids, MI: Discovery House Publishing, 2007), 69–70.
13. Hannah Whitall Smith, *The God of All Comfort* (London: James Nisbet and Co., Limited, 1906), 252–253.

CHAPTER 6: HOPE AFTER LOSS

1. Wayne Hale, "After Ten Years: Working on the Wrong Problem," January 13, 2013, http://waynehale.wordpress.com/2013/01/13/after-ten-years-working-on-the-wrong-problem.
2. Stephen White, "Revealed: NASA Chiefs Didn't Tell Columbia Space Shuttle Crew They Were about to Die," *Daily Record*, February 2, 2013, www.dailyrecord.co.uk/news/uk-world-news/nasa-knew-space-shuttle-columbia-1569567; Gina Sunseri, "Columbia Shuttle Crew Not Told of Possible Problem with Reentry," ABC News, January 31, 2012, http://abcnews.go.com/Technology/columbia-shuttle-crew-told-problem-reentry/story?id=18366185.
3. Eric Lax, *Woody Allen: A Biography* (New York: Da Capo Press, 1991), 26.
4. Kevin J. Gardner, *Faith and Doubt of John Betjeman: An Anthology of Betjeman's Religious Verse* (New York: Continuum International Publishing Group, 2006), 77.
5. Philippe Ariès and Helen Weaver, *The Hour of Our Death: The Classic History of Western Attitudes toward Death over the Last One Thousand Years* (New York: Vintage Books, 1982).
6. Joseph Bayly, *The View from a Hearse* (Elgin, IL: David C. Cook Publishing Co., 1969), 11–12.
7. Eugene O'Kelly, *Chasing Daylight: How My Forthcoming Death Transformed My Life* (New York: McGraw-Hill, 2007), 17–18.
8. S. I. McMillen, MD, and Dr. David E. Stern, MD, *None of These Diseases: The Bible's Health Secrets for the 21st Century* (Grand Rapids, MI: Fleming H. Revell, 2000), 228.
9. Ligon Duncan, *Fear Not!: Death and Afterlife from a Christian Perspective* (Tain, Scotland: Christian Focus, 2008), 24–25.
10. Philo, *Every Good Man Is Free*, 3:22.
11. Ruth Overholtzer, *From Then till Now* (Warrenton, MO: CEF Press, 1990), 130.
12. Nino Lo Bello, *The Incredible Book of Vatican Facts and Papal Curiosities* (New York: Barnes & Noble Books, 1998), 16.

13. The fifth verse of Watts's (untitled) hymn number 112, as found in collections of his hymns.
14. Larry Libby, *Somewhere Angels* (Sisters, OR: Multnomah Books, 1994), 41.
15. Peter J. Marshall, ed., *The Wartime Sermons of Dr. Peter Marshall* (Tulsa, OK: CrossStaff Publishing, 2005).
16. *Perfect Illustrations for Every Topic and Occasion*, compiled by the editors of PreachingToday.com (Carol Stream, IL: Tyndale House Publishers, Inc., 2002), 289.
17. Robert J. Morgan, *The Lord Is My Shepherd* (New York: Howard Books, 2013), 116–117.
18. James M. Campbell, *Heaven Opened* (New York: Revell, 1924), 178.
19. Michael P. Green, ed., *Illustrations for Biblical Preaching* (Grand Rapids, MI: Baker Book House, 1989), 91.
20. Corrie ten Boom, *He Cares, He Comforts* (Old Tappan, NJ: Fleming H. Revell, 1977), 89–90.
21. Franz Liszt, *Les Preludes: Symphonic Poem No. 3* (Van Nuys, CA: Alfred Music Publishing, 1985), 39.
22. C. S. Lewis, *The Last Battle* (New York: Macmillan, 1956), 210–211.
23. Charles L. Allen, *You Are Never Alone* (Old Tappan, NJ: Fleming H. Revell, 1978), 77–79.

CHAPTER 7: YOUR ULTIMATE HOPE

1. C. S. Lewis, *The Silver Chair* (New York: HarperCollins Publishers, 1981), 22–23.
2. Dr. Dan B. Allender and Dr. Tremper Longman III, *The Cry of the Soul: How Our Emotions Reveal Our Deepest Questions about God* (Colorado Springs: NavPress, 1994), 100.
3. Ravi Zacharias, *Can Man Live Without God?* (Dallas: Word Publishing, 1994), 89.
4. Martin Wells Knapp, *Revival Tornadoes: or, Life and Labors of Rev. Joseph H. Weber* (Boston: McDonald, Gill, & Co., 1890), 178.
5. Quoted by Edgar H. Lewellen in *Revival: God's Proven Method of Awakening His Church* (Maitland, FL: Xulon Press, 2005), 10.
6. Wesley L. Duewel, *Revival Fire* (Grand Rapids, MI: Zondervan, 1995), 139–141.
7. Duewel, 139–141.
8. John Piper, *The Pleasures of God* (Sisters, OR: Multnomah Books, 2000), 198–199.

About the Author

Dr. David Jeremiah serves as senior pastor of Shadow Mountain Community Church in El Cajon, California. He is the founder and host of *Turning Point*, a ministry committed to providing Christians with sound Bible teaching relevant to today's changing times through radio and television, the internet, live events, and resource materials and books. A bestselling author, Dr. Jeremiah has written more than forty books, including *Agents of Babylon, Agents of the Apocalypse, Captured by Grace, Living with Confidence in a Chaotic World, What in the World Is Going On?, The Coming Economic Armageddon, God Loves You: He Always Has—He Always Will,* and *What Are You Afraid Of?*

Dr. Jeremiah's commitment to teaching the complete Word of God continues to make him a sought-after speaker and writer. His passion for reaching the lost and encouraging believers in their faith is demonstrated through his faithful communication of biblical truths.

A dedicated family man, Dr. Jeremiah and his wife, Donna, have four grown children and twelve grandchildren.